*W*holing the *H*eart

Good News
for Those
Who Grew Up
in Troubled Families

Rachel Callahan
Rea McDonnell

Islewest
PUBLISHING

Library of Congress Cataloging-in-Publication Data

Callahan, Rachel.
    Wholing the heart: good news for those who grew up in troubled
families / by Rachel Callahan and Rea McDonnell.
        p. cm.
    Includes bibliographical references.
    ISBN 0-8091-3233-8
    1. Psychology, Religious.   2. Family—Psychological aspects.
3. Consolation.   I. McDonnell, Rea.   II. Title
BL53.C323   1991
248.8′6—dc20   91-12036
                                                                          CIP

Published by Islewest Publishing,
4242 Chavenelle Rd., Dubuque, IA 52002
1-800-557-9867
mjgraham@carcomm.com

Printed and bound in the United States of America

ISBN 1-888461-07-1

Contents

In grateful memory of
Mom O'Donnell
and dedicated to our
students and clients

Preface

It is frigid here in Ocean City, Maryland. The shoreline has frozen with thin ice and is littered with shells which are half-filled with frozen salt water. The beach is strewn with shells that have been battered and bruised by the harsh waters of winter. Many of the shells are broken and laced with holes. The same shells, which in summer are usually whole, surprise us with the different amazing beauty of holes and brokenness. The iridescent whorls that hide inside the now broken conch open like lovely shimmering satin and catch the sun in ways that less battered shells could never do. The holes give infinite variety to fairly predictable shape.

This morning a kitten appeared on the porch, shivering in the wind but resting in the warm place where the sun reflects off the ocean in this sub-zero cold. This tiny quivering scrap of fur looked hungry and very cold. Yet to approach it with warm milk, and later with some solid food, caused the kitty to dash away from the sun and food, to dart across the snowy porch to what must have seemed a safer place. Only later, when we were safely out of the way, did the kitten venture warily back, and greedily but furtively lap up the milk. Only later,

1

after much sniffing and backing away, did it finally come near the richer solid food to eat. Whatever impulses we may have had to bring this tiny stray in from the arctic cold were stifled by the kitten's skittish fear of letting us near.

This experience at the winter beach speaks to us of frozen, hungry, skittish hearts. It reminds us that brokenness and holes have their own particular beauty and capacity to reflect and hold the sun. This morning the kitten especially reminds us of how we can be with the God who yearns to feed us and give us warmth and shelter. If life experience has not taught us to trust and respond, we tend to skitter away to what seems to be a safer place. And still God yearns to tame us.

> *Jerusalem, Jerusalem, how I have longed to gather you as a hen gathers her brood.*   —Luke 13:34

Take some time now and listen as God speaks.
Insert your name. Hear God call you by name:

> "_____ _____, *how I have longed to gather you to my heart.*"

"Return to the Land Where You Were Born"

Since the publication of our *Hope for Healing: Good News for Adult Children of Alcoholics,* many readers have told us that much of that book and many of those exercises apply to them, although they could not identify alcoholism in their parents or even grandparents. They instead name their families of origin as "troubled." There are many factors which trouble a family besides alcoholism, even in our culture where basic needs for food, shelter, and relative safety are ordinarily available.

We are born into the community of a family. When we leave home it most often is to create a new community, a new family in which so many of us hope to "do it right," set it straight, and be the ideal parent we were hoping for as youngsters. Many times, however, we actually repeat what we want to make right. Children of alcoholics often become spouses of alcoholics. Victims of abuse can themselves become abusers.

The seeds of troubled families and other troubled communities lie in the unhealed "holes" in the hearts of their members. Too often the "holes" leave us homeless in that most important first home of our own, that is, our very selves. This book is about the movement from "homelessness" to a greater sense of "at-home-ness" within our very selves.

One of the best guarantees of healthy, functional family and community life is the recognition of and respect for each person as a separate self with distinct needs, wants, and feelings. Such families and communities encourage us to be who we are, our true selves. This is what God wants for each of us and all of us. Whether married, single, or single again, whether in religious, work, or civic communities, lest we act out of and hand on the isolation, shame, or pain which we grew up with, it is time for us as adults who grew up in troubled families to hear the good news:

> *"I will take away your hearts of stone and give you hearts of flesh; I will give you a new and healed heart and will put a new spirit within you."* —Ezekiel 11:19

Sigmund Freud argued that our character is fairly well formed by the time we are five years old. Yet life in Christ, in the Spirit, is meant to be a re-forming and trans-forming experience. In this book we hope to explore what in a young child's formation leads to so much distress, even pain, within our adult selves and in our relationships. We will provide some spiritual exercises to invite the Spirit to transform and make whole our hearts, our very selves.

Many of us grow up to be competent, well-functioning adults. To most of the world we look like good parents, friends, teachers, and workers. But inside we experience "holes"—hearts which feel empty, anxious, lonely, and unhappy with the person we have become. We may place unrealistic demands upon ourselves and others and sometimes label these demands as "what God wants."

Where do these "holes" in our hearts originate? Certainly there is the incompleteness which is the grace of simply being human. "Our hearts are made for you, O God, and cannot rest until they rest in you" (*Confessions of St. Augustine*). Some of us, however, carry holes which are deeper and more painful because of our early experiences as children.

Psychological research has confirmed the critical importance of the first two years of life. How well we experience the process of bonding and attachment with the person who acts as mother for us, and how successfully we negotiate those first steps toward becoming separate selves, impacts not only our capacity to form relationships for the rest of our lives, but also our ability to tolerate solitude as a separate self.

There are many reasons why this crucial process of attachment and separation might not happen in the "good enough" fashion necessary for healthy human development: parental illness, such as depression, alcoholism, or severe stress; fatigue associated with too many children; or parental preoccupation with survival of their marriage, their family, their job, and economic stability. These "holes" in our parents' hearts may contribute to our lack of bonding with them or our inability to be separate from them.

If a baby does not receive the *physical* nourishment it needs, the effects are seen in stunted growth, lackluster hair, and other physical signs—some quite severe. With the sad exception of the babies born into abject poverty or into families in which there is severe physical neglect, there is thankfully not too much evidence of the lack of physical nourishment of infants in our culture. The phenomenon of "boarder babies" who never leave the hospital because they have nowhere to go, and of those born addicted to crack and other drugs, may soon make this a more common occurrence.

What about the evidence of insufficient *affective* nourishment and encouragement of the baby to move securely toward development of a separate self? Some of the holes in the adult heart which suggest this lack of emotional nourishment include feelings of not belonging, feelings of not really having a right to exist, and the incapacity to relish the simple joys of being alone and/or in relationship. On the other hand, instead of finding it hard to relate, some adults might be addicted to relationships. We experience an inordinate amount of "attachment hunger" which we may try to hide even from ourselves by excessive care-taking of others. These feelings sometimes are experienced as a deep discomfort with our own needs and a reluctance to try to meet them—a profound conviction, conscious or unconscious, that we have no right to have needs.

Another "hole" which we might experience as adults is feel-ing disappointed with life as it is too much of the time. We may present ourselves to the world as extraordinarily competent, even perfectionistic individuals. But we feel impatient with our own limits and those of others. Inside our very gifted responsible public self is a private self which is excruciatingly vulnerable to feelings of shame, humiliation, worthlessness, and loneliness.

We will further describe these holes in the heart or deficien-cies at the core (*cor* is "heart" in Latin) as we name the frozen heart, the hungry heart, and the frantic heart. We carry these holes not because our parents were bad people. Like the mother whose own malnutrition makes her milk for her baby dry up, our parents, especially the mothering figure, may bear holes in their own hearts which make it difficult to be "good enough" parents. It is hard to give what you do not have. Or perhaps circum-stances of severe stress which coincided with the attachment-sep-aration period in our development left our parents unable to be with us in a "good enough" way for us to negotiate this critical time in our infant lives.

This book is written with the hope that as we understand and place before our God some of these "holes" in our adult hearts, some healing can happen. Our own childhood, whatever it joys and pains, is the only chronological childhood we get. Our bodies and minds have matured but our psyches may still be car-rying the wounds which are left from the deficits in this early process of bonding, attachment, and separation. Often therapy, spiritual direction, and/or other healing relationships help us to uncover and understand the "holes" and facilitate the gradual healing and "whole-ing" of the heart.

Our relationship with God (whatever we call God/Jesus/Spirit/Higher Power) can facilitate the healing. Sometimes a comfort against too much pain, always a gentle, nourishing invitation to personal wholeness, our relationship with God invites us to make ourselves available to the conditions in which healing can happen. Our assumption is that the God who loves us meets us exactly where we are in our developmental journeys.

Starting Points

We repeat the primary assumption: God loves us unconditionally and faithfully, and meets us just where we are in our developmental journeys. Jacob, having cheated his older brother Esau out of his birthright, was called to journey back to the country of his childhood. "The Lord said to Jacob: 'Return to the land where you were born and I will be with you' " (Genesis 31:3). Jacob was afraid, and he continued his crooked ways even on the journey home. He sent gifts ahead to Esau in hope of winning his favor, but Esau was already on the way with four hundred men (Genesis 32:6–22).

That very night, Jacob wrestled with the Lord, an intimate way to relate, even in struggle. The Lord struck his hip and gave him a new name, Israel, the one to be favored forever by God. Like Jacob, we too might limp all our lives, but we are favored, can be forgiven, and freed.

> *As Esau approached, Jacob bowed to the ground seven times. . . . Esau ran to meet his brother, embraced him, and flinging himself on Jacob's neck, kissed him and wept.*

Esau then asked why Jacob had sent gifts ahead. "They were meant to win your favor, my lord," Jacob replied. But Esau assured Jacob that there was no need to placate him. Like Esau, God does not need all the gifts we might send ahead to win favor, nor our abject, fearful prostrations. Instead,

> Then Esau said, "Let us break camp and be on our way.
> I will go at your pace."   —Genesis 33:1–13

God meets us just where we are as we begin, or take again at a deeper level, our journey to the land of our childhood. God embraces us in our fear and crooked ways, and travels with us, at our pace. Our first assumption is that God loves us just as we are.

Our second assumption is that God created us to be whole. "My plans for you are plans of peace, not disaster," God promises (Jeremiah 29:11). The Hebrew word for peace, *shalom*, does not only mean absence of conflict. *Shalom* means wholeness, integrity, health, and well-being. We are meant to be one with all creation, reverencing each creature; we are meant to be at one with all of humankind's families and nations; we are meant to be whole within ourselves. God's plans are for our health and well-being.

Greek philosophers have described the human being as having a body and a soul. When western philosophers through the centuries have split the human being in two, however, those who theologize tend to favor the soul over the body. Heresies of the early church, those in Augustine's time and the more modern Jansenism, proclaim how evil the human body and human flesh are, how the body must be denied, subdued and killed so the soul can rise free to divine heights. This scorn for the human body with its sensation, emotions, memory, and imagination is in direct contrast to God's reverence and love for our human flesh. The word of God, after all, took flesh and consecrated all of what it means to be human. The human being—fully human, fully alive—is the glory of God, wrote St. Irenaeus, to combat some of those early heresies (c. A.D. 180).

Israel's theologians, on the other hand, would claim that we do not have a body and a spirit, but that we *are* body-spirit. In this book we will be shaped by the Hebrew understanding of the human person as a spirited body. Heart, our topic, for biblical writers is at the core (*cor:* "heart") of being human. Heart is both of the body, although no mere organ, muscle, or blood-pump, and of the spirit through which we express our self: our mind, will, emotion, memory, and imagination. "For the Hebrews, the heart was not only the source of feelings, desires and thought, but also the very center of the spirit's activities in each person," writes Joseph Grassi (*Healing the Heart,* p. 20). Thus we might paraphrase Jeremiah 29:11: "My plans for you and for your heart are plans of peace, *shalom,* plans for your integrity, for the wholeness of your heart." God's will and hope and passionate desire is for the wholing of our hearts.

A third assumption is biblical. The Second Vatican Council's decree on scripture noted that we find revealed in scripture not historical, scientific, or biographical truth, but that truth which is necessary for our salvation. When we use scripture passages in hope of God's healing, we are using them neither bitterly nor critically, but as symbols with many meanings, as God's word for us.

With a kind of "second naiveté" described by philosopher Paul Ricoeur, we lay aside the historical-critical method of interpretation to let simple stories illuminate our stories, to let words of passion and imagination heal our passion and memories. Scripture is a document of faith, a record of other people's experience with God. There is power in this word to lead us to experience God for ourselves as we read it and pray with it, treasuring it in our hearts.

When the word takes root in our hearts, as we reflect on it like Mary (Luke 2:19, 51), it creates in us all that God wants it to do for us.

> *As rain and snow penetrate the earth, bringing forth fruit
> . . . so my word goes forth from my mouth and does not
> return to me empty, but accomplishes all it was sent to do,
> says the Lord.* —Isaiah 55:10–11

Thus, when we hear or read about Jesus healing the blind, it is our blindness which this powerful word of God heals. If, in a gospel story, a paralyzed person walks, some paralyzed part of us is freed as we take in and digest the gospel word which accomplishes all that God wants for us. The word of God, scripture, does what it says. Because God is a living word, scripture accomplishes in the here and now what it once did in the life of Israel, the life of Jesus, the life of the early church. The word "is not far away in the heavens . . . but very near to you, already in your hearts" (Deuteronomy 30:12–14).

A fourth assumption is that the God we meet in scripture and in the flesh, Jesus, wants to save us in community. We are born into the community of a family. We often repeat that need for our first community, even if our family of origin experience was painful, when we choose our friends, our mate, our co-workers, our church, or our parish. Sometimes, quite unconsciously, we find ourselves relating to our employers, our ministers, or other authorities in some of the same ways we related to our parents.

As we become more healed, wholed, and freed, we will even more need a community for support of our healing. This book is designed to be read and prayed with personally. It will better serve you, however, if you can find at least one member of the community to share some of the sorrow and joy it evokes in you. You may ask a spouse, friend, or sibling to listen; you may prefer a professional helper such as a spiritual director, pastoral counselor, or therapist. We do encourage you, when it is safe enough for you, to share your healing process with at least one other.

Our final assumption is that every human being needs mothering. We are carried in the womb, sometimes with joy, sometimes with distress, and are brought forth out of pain. We have survived.

The child described in Ezekiel 16:1–5 was not mothered but cast out on the ground to die:

> *On the day you were born, your navel cord was uncut, you were not washed, not anointed, not rubbed with salt, not wrapped in swaddling clothes. No one looked on you with compassion nor cared for you. You were instead thrown out on the ground as a loathsome thing and exposed on the day you were born.*

God finds this small creature, rejected and abandoned on the road in Ezekiel 16:6–7:

> *Then I passed by you and saw you struggling in your own blood. I said to you: Live in your blood and thrive, grow like a plant in the field.*

Whether fairly isolated for a while in an incubator, or perhaps not welcomed too joyously, we were at least brought to a home, to some semblance of a family, and someone tended, however minimally, our physical needs. We will call this person from now on "the mothering figure." He or she may be parent, nurse, grandparent, older sibling, or hired help, but someone let us live.

We do not want to engage in mother-bashing. As we asserted in *Hope for Healing*, our book for adult children of alcoholics, our parents are good people, in that case crippled by the disease of alcoholism. If our mothering figure was herself crippled by personal deficits, we do not cast a stone. Our own deficits have twisted us as adults and we have undoubtedly at times handed on our pain to our friends and enemies, children and parents. Our hope is for acceptance of the reality of this human condition: we are hurt and hurting; we too hurt others. God so loved us in this human cycle of pain that God sent a child to embrace the human condition and snap the cycle of heartbreak. Jesus comes to bring into one new family all the scattered and broken children of God (John 11:53).

In Conclusion

We ask you to remember that the healing and "whole-ing" of our hearts is usually not a once-and-for-all event. Like any developmental process it takes time. The progress of wholing is spiral, ever circling deeper into new and more profound places of the heart. Hopefully, your awareness and healing can be deepened as we experience over and over the nurturing acceptance and love of our God. We begin this book by begging the Spirit to open and fill each person who reads it.

Part 1

The Holes
in the Heart

"The Lord is close to the broken-hearted and those who are crushed in spirit, God saves" (Psalm 34). Our hearts may be broken, ravaged, scarred, and empty, but scripture proclaims this good news: God is very close to us in our broken-heartedness. Some of us, however, may have little experience of God's closeness. Like the skittish kitten, we may long for God's warmth and nourishment but are too afraid to let God come close. "God heals the broken-hearted and binds up all their wounds" (Psalm 147). How can we come to know this?

God invites us to pay attention to our hearts, the very source of our being, the core of our humanity. God invites us, like Israel, to return continually to our beginnings. For Israel it was the experience of being formed as a people in a desert journey; for us it is the experience of "being knit in our mother's womb, secretly, wonderfully made" (Psalm 139). Like Israel, loved because it was the smallest of nations (Deuteronomy 7:7–8), so we are tended by God because we were—and still are—so small. Israel celebrates its origins—in fear and slavery, in complaints and contrariness—each year at Passover. Our origins—our holes and hungers, our fears and fusions, slaveries and skittishness, cravings and complaints—attract God to us, not to rescue us but to save us.

Some of our problem with God is that very lack of rescue. We longed to be plucked out of danger and pain. Instead, God saves (in Hebrew, *yesh*). From Israel's own experience in the beginning with God, they saw, heard, tasted, and touched that God's saving meant freedom. To be saved in the Hebrew language means to be given space, to be set free in the open. Israel's freedom led them to the wilderness, a desert of forty years. They often yearned for the security of slavery in Egypt. Yet God "was giving them a home to live in. . . . God bears our burdens day after day. Our God is a God who saves" (Psalm 68).

15

As we return to our origins—in the womb, in our first months, in our early years—we face our own wilderness. Instead of a pillar of fire to guide us, we have an interior gift to lead us: The spirit of truth who will "not leave you orphaned" (John 14:18), Jesus promised. We return to our origins, our home, our hearts, equipped with the Spirit of truth and led by Jesus who knows in his flesh what we have been through. We will explore the gaping holes in our hearts and hopefully uncover some smaller gashes and bruises which may have been long hidden. Although we have divided the infant's developmental stages neatly into three, with corresponding deficits in development which we call "holes," human growth is never so neat. "Stages" may conceal as much truth as they reveal. Instead we may discover parts of us which are frozen, uncover some deeply buried hungers, or claim a characteristic of the frantic heart as our own. There may be a more tidy "fit" into one type of heart-hole, but reality is a mix, an overlap, a spiraling ever deeper into what we thought we already knew, what we thought had already been healed.

Healing and wholing is a lifelong process. It will probably not be neat, nor move steadily through stages. About all we can be sure of is that God is close to those with wounded hearts; that Jesus, whose very name, Yeshua, means saving, does not rescue us but is with us on our journey to health and wholeness; that the Spirit who lives and acts always within our hearts leads us gradually to truth and wholeness and peace.

The Frozen Heart

Come, Spirit of light and warmth. Melt the frozen. Warm the chill (from the hymn Veni Creator).

In this chapter you will be invited to hold before God (or Jesus or the Spirit or however you name God) whatever space in your heart is frozen or chilled. As you begin the chapter we ask you to take an ice cube in your hand.

> Hold the ice cube and *notice* as it melts. Ask God to teach you what you need to experience *right now*. As the warmth of your hand melts the ice you may notice that your hand tingles or even hurts a little. As the ice cube melts it is a little messy. That is how it is with

melting. As the frozen places in your heart start to melt you may experience this as painful and messy. Ask to trust that God is with you and will let you experience only as much as you can bear.

Have you ever studied a frozen lake or pond? Maybe you have a favorite place which is close to water. The stream or the lake, which in summer dances with life and light and motion, in winter gets frozen over and covered with thick white ice. Maybe a log or a stick protrudes, but there is no hint of the life which might be teeming underneath. The wonderful fluid dance of water is temporarily stilled and paralyzed. Maybe the ice is so thick that it can support the weight of a person. Often it is cracked and thin.

When we speak of the frozen heart it is a bit like the winter pond or lake. Somehow the life and vitality is locked in. The heart is the symbol and metaphor for life and love. So when we speak of the frozen heart we are describing the pain which arises from being cut off from the juice and joy of living and loving. Our hearts begin to freeze as children when, in order to survive, we need to cut ourselves off from feelings, desires, and awareness, from the child's delicious sense of spontaneous curiosity, creativity, and enjoyment.

Very often the frozen heart of the adult is filled with a profound sense of shame, some radical sense that at the core of his or her being something is wrong. The world is not experienced as a safe and friendly place. People and relationships are not to be trusted. Too often the frozen heart protects us from that empty sense of not belonging. We are frozen with doubts that we have a right to exist. This painful state of *being* is too unbearable, so we need to take refuge in *doing*. Work and achievement become much safer havens than relationship. The head is definitely a safer place than the heart. To feel would be to hurt, so feeling gets frozen over by denial and by intellectualization.

In this process of freezing over, we reduce some of the feelings of pain. At the same time, however, the capacity to enjoy life in some of its simplest and most elemental moments also gets blocked out. Not only the awareness of feelings but even the awareness of bodily sensations is curtailed so that some of the most simple pleasures of sight, sound, smell, taste, and touch are not developed and enjoyed.

Sometimes a person with a frozen heart experiences feelings of generalized anxiety. Feelings of nervousness, worry, or apprehension, especially in social situations, interfere with the risk of getting to know another. Sometimes the frozen heart makes us feel detached even from ourselves. We become observers of life instead of living it. We stand outside ourselves, watching ourselves.

Unfortunately there are many physical dimensions of anxiety which mimic bodily illness. These can be frightening enough to keep a person even more cautious about living. Heart palpitations, light-headedness, diarrhea, or feeling a lump in the throat can further deter us from enjoying life. The world is experienced as a dangerous place, not to be trusted or enjoyed.

In the Beginning . . .

In the beginning . . . something interferes with the crucial process of attachment and bonding. The newborn's first experience of the world, instead of being a warm and welcoming one, is a rejecting or disinterested one. Maybe the baby is not wanted. Maybe the mother is incapable of welcoming the child either because of her own deficits or because of some physical or psychological reason. Maybe the responsibilities of caring for this tiny scrap of totally helpless and dependent humanity are too much. Maybe the baby is a disappointment, sickly, deformed, or colicky. For whatever reason, that early crucial process of bonding does not happen.

The baby may itself be incapable of bonding. One of the things we know about this early process of attachment is that some infants do not have the capacity to respond to mothering. Bonding depends upon the good fit between the baby's signals of needs and the mother's adequate response to these. If a baby does not signal the distress of being wet, cold, or hungry, the mother may not know of the infant's pain.

During the first six months of life it is critical that the baby receive not only food and comfort but also enough tender holding so as to begin to experience the world as a friendly and safe place. In these early months the mothering figure needs to provide a holding environment in order for an infant to thrive and grow. " 'Holding' is everything that happens to an infant which sustains her and produces wholeness and integration" (Louise Kaplan, *Oneness and Separateness: From Infant to Individual*, p. 91). When the bonding during these early months is "good enough" the baby experiences that blissful state of oneness and safety, being understood and responded to. Whether the need for holding has been met or not, the need remains in our preverbal feeling-memory as a memory trace of either bliss or acute yearning.

During these early months a baby has no clear sense of boundaries between mother and its tiny self. From the infant's vantage point the boundaries between mother and self are nonexistent. Consequently, the infant is very vulnerable to absorbing the mother's tensions, fears, anxieties, angers, joys, and sorrows. He shares totally in her moods.

During these early months it is natural for an infant to "mold" to its mother. Its tiny body curves, snuggles, and nuzzles to fit the comforting contours of the mother's breast, lap, and shoulder. When a baby is in distress its natural movement is to stiffen. The tiny screaming infant is often rigid in its pain, resisting the comfort of the parent's holding.

But what happens if an infant's pain comes not from internal distress of gas or hunger but from outside the self, from the mother? If the attachment process gets disrupted, whether by unconscious or by overt rejection from the mothering figure, the infant is at great risk. If the rejection continues or even becomes outright abuse as the baby grows, the infant learns to freeze feelings. The same stiffening which is the early physical response to body-pain becomes the emotional response of freezing feelings.

There are so many factors which may disrupt the process of attachment. Loss of a spouse through death, divorce, or long separation; any significant family, especially parental, illness or early hospitalization of the child; economic strain—all these factors can upset family balance in such a way that the environment for the baby is hostile rather than safe. A baby's natural response to a cold and hostile environment is terror and rage. Since this is a very unsafe way to survive early on, the baby learns to cut off feeling and withdraw, in a very real way to "stop living." Gradually the child cuts him or herself off from his/her own experience in order to be protected from feeling overwhelming pain, loss, and shame. Thus the freezing process begins. Gradually the heart and the spirit of the tiny child hardens in order to survive. Very often this infant starts to inhibit both movement and breathing, which may persist even to adulthood. The person has "stiffened" internally.

However, these babies can grow up to be competent adults. They discover early on that the world of the mind and the world of achievement are much safer havens in which to dwell than the totality of life with all the messiness of vitality. Denial, the over-arching defense in any troubled family system, is well entrenched. The aching script that "there is something wrong with me" needs to be defended against not only by denial but sometimes as well by intellectualization—keeping a strict wall between what goes on in our heads and the rest of our sensing-feeling experience.

> Perhaps as you read this you recognize yourself. If there is a frozen hole in your heart created by this early experience of parental deprivation, you might want to stop reading this. Please honor your feeling, your desire to stop. Lay this book aside. Do some relaxed, deep breathing. Instead of turning to a familiar escape, however, try to turn to some space or activity which feels safe and comforting to you: reading, taking a walk, perhaps imagining a favorite

spot or paging through a picture album of a treasured vacation.

You may never pick up this book again. You are worth the few dollars spent on it. You may wait till you feel better about yourself or until you have found a therapist or until your friend returns for a visit. Remember, God goes at our pace. God can heal you in a few moments, whereas, for others, God might use years of therapy. There is no better way, just your unique response to God's desire for your *shalom:* peace, healing, and wholeness.

If you want to continue using this book, we invite you to repeat the prayer exercise with the ice cube which was suggested at the beginning of the chapter. Picture the ice cube as your own heart. Hold the frozen parts of your heart gently before God. Try to feel and to trust the slow, painful healing from frozen to feeling.

"Come, Holy Spirit! Melt the frozen, warm the chill."

2

The Hungry
Heart

You satisfy the hungry heart . . .

In this chapter you are invited to share your hungers with God, a God who is sympathetic to hunger. "Oh, if only you would open your mouth, I would feed you the finest wheat and satisfy you with honey from the rock" (Psalm 81), God cries. Whether it is the rasping gnaw of physical hunger which afflicts so many in our world, or the more subtle growl of spiritual and psychological hunger which moves so many in our society to become addicts, God longs to satisfy these hungers, longs to feed us. In Luke's gospel, Jesus in his sermon on the plain proclaims:

> *"Happy you who are hungry now; you shall be satisfied."* —Luke 6:21

Take a few minutes and write down the hungers within you which you can name. Perhaps acceptance or recognition is your craving, perhaps a sense of belonging or being special to someone.

After you have thought and remembered, quiet your mind and let the Spirit reveal from deep within you. Ask the Spirit to show you where your heart is hungry, confident that our God invites you:

Oh, come to the water all you who are thirsty; though you have no money, come! Buy corn without money and eat, and at no cost, wine and milk. . . . Why spend your money . . . for what fails to satisfy? Listen, listen to me, and you will have good things to eat and rich food to enjoy.
—Isaiah 55:1–2

Now, show God (Jesus/Spirit) your list of hungers. You might sit a while with your mouth open, saying in your heart. Feed me.

The United States is a hungry society. The last few decades witnessed great attention to the various phenomena of addiction, both substance and process addictions. Recovery programs and support groups have multiplied, but not quickly enough to stem some of the tides of addiction in society. Unfortunately the advertising industry creates hungers even where they do not exist and stimulates wants and cravings.

In the Beginning . . .

We all need a sense of belonging, of being connected, of care and approval. The inordinate craving for care and approval which can cripple us as adults, however, comes not from Madison Avenue but from early experiences of inconsistency and deprivation in the infant's process of attachment. Attachment to the mothering figure, described in the previous chapter, continues during the first year of life. A baby has the right to existence and so much more. The infant's needs for nurturance, sustenance, and touch must be met fairly consistently or else the baby is going to experience a feeling of abandonment.

When mothering needs are met in what D. W. Winnicott, the British psychiatrist/author, calls "good enough" ways, the baby experiences that magical world in which "Mommy and I are one." For babies successfully to negotiate this critical passage of attachment on the way to becoming tiny separate selves, they need one steady, emotionally available mother figure who takes care of their basic needs in a consistent enough way.

During the first few months of life, a baby does not seem to recognize and/or mind the mother's absence so long as its needs get met. By the eighth month, however, that changes. Mother is recognized, the infant is attached to *this* one. Babies become terribly upset if Mommy or their primary attachment figure stays absent too long. Separation anxiety, which plagues many fully functioning adults, has begun.

At about six months, however, the baby itself is beginning to separate. A baby starts to differentiate and become a separate self. The urges to leave the lap are felt more acutely. At the beginnings of separateness, it is still critical that Mommy be available in a consistent way. This is when the baby's specific smile of recognition for Mommy or howl of protest around strangers signals that the baby both knows and needs its particular mothering figure.

Mommies are not God. Their faithfulness is flawed. Mothers can be chronically ill, depressed, or alcoholic. External circumstances also interfere with their availability on demand. Like Martha of the gospel, they have to be busy about many things, and some mothers cannot rest, organize, and prioritize. A mother's concern about economic problems, rage at an unjust boss or an absent spouse, worry about a child-abusing or drug-abusing spouse, concern about older children or elderly parents, or just the day-to-day crises of family life create frustrations for the wailing infant who wants Mommy now. Even Winnicott's "good enough mother" is flawed. Even she is not God.

Babies adjust and accommodate to this real disappointment or to real or perceived abandonment because chronic upset is too painful to endure. With no sense of real time, infants experience hours or even minutes as lasting for an eternity. Babies then shut down their own needs to protect themselves from feeling abandoned. John Bowlby, a British psychiatrist, outlines this process in the second volume of his *Attachment and Loss*, entitled *Separation: Anxiety and Anger*. We can easily, if less scientifically, observe the process with the infants around us.

When a baby of this age is left for some time by its mother, it wails desperately, then appears to give up and adjust to the separation. When Mommy returns, instead of joyful reunion there is some strain and restraint. The child holds back its trust. Baby appears not to need or even not to want the mother for a while.

Developmentally this feeling of abandonment occurs during that time when babies are starting to enjoy their love affair with the world. Everything becomes on object of wonder and delight to be touched, tasted, or examined. From about ten to fifteen months, as a baby climbs down from Mommy's lap, there is so much to explore. Babies enjoy the new delight of mobility— scooting, then crawling, and eventually upright locomotion, walking, and running almost on tiptoe. Yet they keep checking back with Mommy, at least by glance if not by actual physical return. This is a time of both grandiosity and vulnerability. The baby needs both the opportunity to practice its newly discovered autonomy and the chance to swing back to the dependence of vulnerable babyhood. The toddler still needs to enjoy being the twinkle in Mommy's eye and yet needs the opportunity to experiment with separateness.

There are at least two ways in which this attachment-separation movement can be marred. Both paradoxically result in what Howard Halpern, clinical psychologist and author, labels "attachment hunger." For some of the reasons cited earlier in this chapter the mother can be too unavailable for the child. On the other hand, however, she can be too available, hovering, having trouble letting go of the infant. Wanting to keep her baby, whether physically or at least symbolically, on the lap or at the breast, she is uneasy with the autonomous explorations of her toddler. Admittedly, open stairways, exposed electrical outlets, and other potential hazards such as cupboards and drawers not yet "childproofed" can become heart stoppers if the tot gets too close to real danger.

Sometimes it is not physical danger which causes mothers to cling, but their own insecurities or needs to keep an infant attached even when the time comes to separate. Mothers can be addicted to their infants, feeling their own grandiosity as sole supports of the weak, defenseless little ones. The toddler's need to be independent threatens the mother's self-image, her role as all-powerful caretaker.

The delicate balancing act between respecting a child's natural grandiosity and need for autonomy, and yet respecting the toddler's genuine vulnerability, is a real challenge. The mood swings of this age group can be overwhelming; they call for a steadiness in the parents, a sense of being rooted in their own relatively whole selves, of being able to count on the steady love of the spouse. This parenting need not be perfect, just good enough.

If, as infants, we have not successfully negotiated this passage of attachment to separation we are apt to grow up with either "attachment hunger" or with a need to deny our own neediness. Attachment hunger is a powerful, preverbal, feeling-memory. It may be triggered by the loss, real or anticipated, of a significant figure in our adult life. This hunger is experienced as an extremely needy vulnerability and clinging. It may look like possessiveness, addiction to a person. Like the early feeling experience of being left for what seemed like forever as infants, as adults we feel as though "I can't live without him or her."

This attachment hunger creates a fear not only of being left, but also of leaving. We cling even to harmful relationships as adults for fear of abandonment. This is the basis of relationship addiction and co-dependence. It evokes a feeling level for which we may not even have words—the memory of parents being physically or emotionally absent at a time when, at least psychologically, the baby literally could not live without them.

The other heritage of being left at this critical time is the denial of legitimate neediness. The baby, whose mother is not there repeatedly, learns to accommodate and to contract against its own need. To create the illusion of not needing is less painful than continued frustration of needs. Learning self-sufficiency as quickly as possible, the little person grows into an adult whose fundamental attitude is still dependency, but dependency gone underground. This shameful, childish dependency must be kept hidden, even from oneself. The longing for a "special someone" and subsequent disappointment even to the point of despair gets transformed into the much safer psychological terrain of giving and caring. Too often habits of poor self-care and overextension lead to exhaustion and sometimes illness which seems the only legitimate way to need and to get cared for.

Deep within us is the hunger for the old "paradise lost," that symbiotic union in which "Mommy and I are one." That hunger for attachment is well camouflaged as the kind of caretaking which keeps co-dependent spouses, friends, employees, and family members locked into unhealthy relationships. So much of the popular literature on co-dependence describes the adult whose own need is denied and projected onto others. The projection of our neediness onto others lets us fool ourselves that we are not the needy ones; they are. Of course, that leaves us in a "one-up" position, a position of disrespect so profound that some authors call it contempt (Alice Miller, *The Drama of the Gifted Child*; John Patton, *Is Human Forgiveness Possible?*). The underlying fear remains that exposure of our own neediness even to ourselves will result in our being despised and abandoned—again.

The invitation for the hungry heart is precisely the invitation to expose our neediness to the God who neither despises us nor could ever abandon us. "Listen to me, Yahweh, and answer me, poor and needy as I am" (Psalm 86:1). We believe that "the Lord hears the cry of the poor" and yet can so easily forget our own emotional poverty, the hole of heart-hunger which gnaws and throbs in pain.

> *The poor and needy ask for water, and there is none, their tongue is parched with thirst. I, Yahweh, will answer them. I, the God of Israel, will not abandon them.*
> —Isaiah 41:17

Yes, there is a real economic poverty, actual physical famine and starvation in our ghettos and hollers as well as abroad. Yet attention to others' needs while blinding our eyes to our own may engender more contempt than compassion. To refuse to see our own neediness because the needs of the economically poor so consume us usually leads to the disaster of burnout. As co-dependent rescuers we can soon slide into persecuting and oppressing others when our own needs are not attended to. From RE-pression of ourselves to OP-pression of others may be a short step. There is no need for an either/or stance here: *either* my healing *or* their well-being. God has time and energy to save us both. God has heart-room for us all.

> *Does a woman forget her baby at the breast, or fail to cherish the child of her womb? Yet even if these forget, I will never forget you. . . . I have carved you on the palms of my hands.* —Isaiah 49:15–16

3

The Frantic Heart

My heart is longing for your peace . . . like a weaned child on its mother's lap.

In this chapter we will attend to those frantic places in the heart—those driving anxieties which make us rely on achievement and perfectionism, those places in the heart where shame and self-depreciation tyrannize us with unreal expectations of ourselves and others. This frantic requirement to do it right, to be right, to have it right, and to get it right, too often blocks our enjoying the ordinary but sometimes ragged edges of reality. We are left vulnerable to feeling disappointed or let down by those who fail to notice and applaud all our efforts and standards. The frantic heart is too often agitated by criticism of self and others, irritated with others who fail to meet their expectations and desires of how they and the world "should" be.

If you are achievement-oriented, go and find your date book or the calendar on which you mark family events or work appointments. Review your past month. Where have you gone? At what pace have you gone? How are you feeling about your commitments? What do you want? What do you need? Why do you do all that you do? And how do you feel about that?

Hold your calendar, your month, and all your feelings before God. Insert your name in the blank and hear God say: "Come to me, _____, you who are so heavy-burdened. I want to give you rest."

In the Beginning . . .

As with the two "holes" we have already described, let us examine the origins of the "frantic" heart. Sometimes children are treated as an extension of their parents. We may have been required to be the way they wanted us to be rather than the way we naturally and uniquely are. Instead of fostering a tiny emerging true self, parents sow the seeds for the development of our false self with its frantic heart. Our false self is a human doing rather than a human being.

Alice Miller, the Swiss psychoanalyst and author of *The Drama of the Gifted Child* (originally published in 1979 as *Prisoners of Childhood*), has done so much to further our understanding of non-physical child abuse and the development of the false self. She describes the gifted child who many of us may have been—the pride of our parents, capable, competent. We may have been the center of their attention, grandiose in our performances as toddlers and two-year-olds. Inside, however, we were becoming plagued by anxiety or stifled by deep feelings of shame and guilt.

When children are used to gratify and complete their parents' sense of themselves they tend to develop the "false self." They are required to be and act a certain way at the expense of the "true self" with its great range and depth of feelings, desires, and expressions of the unique self.

Between the ages of fifteen and twenty-four months the child is especially vulnerable to the development of a false self. We make a spontaneous gesture, writes Winnicott, and it is corrected. We offer a new word which we are trying out and we are ridiculed. We have an original thought and our parents feel threatened by the emerging of a separate self. We are thwarted, cut off in our creativity, bent and shaped to our parents' needs or family traditions or cultural/religious standards or . . . or . . . We are becoming not our own self, but the self that others, the most essential others, want us to be.

As we climb off the lap, our first attempt at selfhood, it is the first time as humans that we begin to integrate both the magnificence and the vulnerability which is the glory of the human person. This emerges in both tender and trying ways for parents. The toddler has found new power. An imperious "No" rings out. This is not simply the negativity of a two-year-old who acts as "His (or Her) Majesty, the Baby." This "No" is a declaration of the emerging reality of separateness.

What if the "No" is not tolerated? What if the child's grandiosity, natural for that age, is too quickly deflated or the toddler's genuine vulnerability is exploited by parents who use the child to give them a sense of accomplishment? What if the parents require the child to be or behave a certain way in order to maintain parental love and approval?

Since children need parental love and approval in order to survive, let alone thrive, we soon learn to accommodate to parental requirements. Children this age still need the mirroring which allows them to see that they are the "twinkle in Mommy's eye"—just the way they are. In order to confront the vulnerability of being human they need to borrow from the strength of their parents in an idealized way.

At first the mother is all good, all satisfying, the ideal mother, as the baby experiences her. Quickly the baby splits: the mother is *all* good or *all* bad. In later stages of development, the child begins to internalize that Mommy can be both good (satisfying) *and* bad (withholding or punitive). Not only "can be" but is. This taking in of a mother who is both/and rather than either/or keeps a child from getting snared and stuck in the primitive defense of splitting. "Splitting" here means that parents are perceived as all good or all bad. What was meant to be a stage of development freezes into a permanent worldview—and a permanent, if waffling, self-understanding. Our self-concept as adults may be split, may swing between grandiosity with illusions of power, and then, utter self-contempt. If the child can develop the capacity to experience something or someone as both good and not good at the same time, then that child will grow into an adult who will be able to see, accept, even embrace reality and the reality of the self in all of its rich shades, with all of its ragged edges.

In order to accommodate to parental needs, children learn to develop what Miller refers to as an "as-if personality," what Winnicott labels the "false self." The false self is the person the world meets—perfectionistic, grandiose, and entitled. This adult is often manipulative; having been used by parents to meet their needs, he or she knows no other way to relate with others. Inside this adult, however, dwells a private self whom no one knows. This private self feels vulnerable to shame and humiliation, worthless, often isolated, and lonely. Meanwhile the "true self" which has never had the chance, or only minimally, to develop and grow often feels empty and fragmented. Its creativity, spontaneity, originality, full range of emotion, needs, and wants lie buried beneath the requirements, standards, and dreams of others.

Now, as an adult, the anger which one needed to "kill" as a child bubbles up in irritation (often quite intense) and disap-

pointment at how life and people and society and church and
. . . and . . . really are. This profound disappointment effective-
ly blocks the enjoyment of life in its ordinariness and the appreciation of others as separate persons. Just as these adults were
required to be, think, feel, and behave a certain way as children,
they now unconsciously maintain the same requirement of others.

When a child has to choose to develop the false self at the
expense of the emerging true self, the price tag is the experience
of childhood itself. The well-behaved, reliable, understanding,
compliant youngster, some as young as a year old, who learns to
key in to parental wants and requirements never or seldom gets
the chance to be a full self. Since it was not safe to show one's parents, relatives, and neighbors the ugly, angry, jealous, lazy, dirty,
smelly child which every human youngster really is (as well as
cute and competent), the false-self child needed to hide the true
self from parents and eventually even from self.

In troubled families, this child kept the parents feeling adequate, perhaps even proud of themselves and their product. This
child was undoubtedly but unconsciously assigned a family
role(s), perhaps even at this early age. Then, whatever tenuous
balance existed in the family would not be threatened. This child
acted "as if" being Daddy's little princess, Mommy's little helper,
the family entertainer, or the "brain" gave her/him meaning and
value.

Frantic to survive, to win approval, to succeed, to shine, this
child becomes the adult whose frantic heart, with its holes gaping empty, hopes for wholing, *shalom*, peace. "My heart is longing for your peace, near to you my God. I do not busy myself
with things too sublime for me" (Psalm 131). Like weaned children on their mothers' laps, the frantic long for peace.

Part 2

Wholing the Heart

In the Anglo-Saxon language, *heal, health,* and *whole* share the same root. Healing the heart is wholing the heart. As God promised, a whole heart will be a heart of flesh (Ezekiel 11:19). God seems to delight in flesh, in what is human, in what is of the earth. God wanted to experience a heart of flesh, and so God's Word became flesh and lived, laughed, and loved among us.

Jesus came among us, rocked in the womb, feeling the warmth, safety, and continual nourishment from his mother. He heard her steady heartbeat and was comforted by its pulse.

One night, as Luke and Matthew tell us, Jesus was thrust out into the cold. He was choked into a narrow space and was terrified as his mother's steady pulse pushed him away. Our word *anxiety* stems from *angostos,* a narrowness. Jesus suffered like us in this birth anxiety—and not only his own anxiety. This baby would have shared, as we do, the anxieties of his mother. He would also have picked up non-verbally the anxiety of Joseph who may never have delivered a living creature before. He wailed in terror. Thus begins the gospel, the good news that Jesus is like us in all things.

The Word becomes flesh—full of grace and truth (John 1:14, 17). Grace is, in Hebrew, the word *hesed,* a word with many meanings, a word which is a name for God's own self. *Hesed* means grace, kindness, tenderness, compassion, and mercy—a love which is abundant, extravagant, and unconditional. Truth is *'emet* in Hebrew, often linked with *hesed* as another name for God. *'Emet* means truth, fidelity, steadfastness—a devotion which is steady, consistent, unfailing, forever, and everlasting. God is known in the Jewish scriptures as *hesed* and *'emet,* and now Jesus has put flesh on God's steady, faithful, unconditional love for us.

God's *hesed* and *'emet* are so healing, providing a faithful presence and availability, a tender caring for our needs, and an unconditional love which sets us free to be our own true selves. Again and again, God tried to communicate to us this kind of motherly compassion. The opening line of the letter to the Hebrews instructs us: "In times past God spoke in so many different ways to our ancestors through the prophets"—prophets who cried "Comfort, give comfort to my people" (Isaiah 40:1). It is often hard for us to trust God's consolation and compassion. Hebrews thus continues: "In these last days God spoke to us through a son . . . who is the fullness of God's glory, the image of all who God is" (Hebrew 1:1–3). God's glory is Jesus—in the flesh. Jesus puts flesh on God's *hesed* and *'emet,* God's faithful love for us.

The glory of God is the human being fully alive, wrote St. Irenaeus, bishop of Lyon, about a century after Hebrews was written. Jesus is our pioneer (Hebrew 12:2) in becoming fully human. As he grew in wisdom, age, and grace (Luke 2:40, 52) he was becoming more totally human, of the earth, more and more fully alive. What God has done with and for Jesus, the first-born of many brothers and sisters, God wants to do with and for us. God passionately desires that we become not angels, not divine, but fully human, fully alive, whole. The way to healing and wholeness is to become more and more human.

Healing is a beautiful, deep, spiritual experience, but also a lifelong process. In the process, healing will be painful, sad, enraging, frightening, and messy. God goes at our pace and has no need to hurry us toward wholeness. God does not need us to look good.

Alice Miller describes a gifted child, "small and lonely, hidden behind his achievements," who asks his parents: "If I had appeared before you, bad, ugly, angry, jealous, lazy, dirty, smelly? Where would your love have been then? And I was all these things as well" (p. 15). To our small and lonely questioning of God: "Do you want me, do you love me all full of pain, sadness, rage, terror, and mess?" God offers a resounding *Yes!*

Because God knows, in the very gut of Jesus, how painful it feels to be rejected, betrayed, abandoned, and used, God does passionately desire our healing. Yet God does not wait for the finished product: the healed heart. God goes with us and within us, whether we step forward, sideward, or backward, even if we just sit down in our tracks and refuse to budge.

We ask you to create in your inner space a safe place for sitting, for refusing, for waiting, for resting, and for retreating. It seems that only once in our lifetime do we get such an ultimately safe space. We are in the womb. At a point when our fetal brains have developed enough, we become conscious of our mother's breath and heartbeat, our own comfort, and our parents' voices. Newborns, in experiments, placed in a room with a group of men, turn instinctively toward their own father's voice—provided the father has been near during the pregnancy, of course. As newborns we are comforted at the breast not only by warm milk but by the familiar breath and heartbeat of the mother as well (Grassi, pp. 10–17). We are reassured by the familiar voices of our parents.

Early in Israel's relationship with God, God offered the people a safe space, a place of womb-like safety, warmth, and nourishment. God called this space within God's own self, within God's own heart, compassion. God's compassion is a sacred space in which we can grow toward new birth. God offers us today a womb-compassion.

Once Moses begged God: "Let me see your glory." God responded (and responds to us): "I will make all my beauty pass before you" (Exodus 33:18–19). God then proclaims a new and more relational name than the name Yahweh ("I am who I am"—Exodus 3:14). God cries out: "The Lord, the Lord, a compassionate and gracious God, slow to anger and rich in kindness (*hesed*) and fidelity (*'emet*)" (Exodus 34:6). The word "compassionate," in this new name for God, is *rachum* in Hebrew. *Rachum* shares the same root, *r ch m*, as the word *rechem*. *Rechem* is the Hebrew word for womb. God's compassion is then a womb-compassion, a kindness which meets us and forms us in the womb. "You knit me in my mother's womb; I give you thanks that I am wonderfully made" (Psalm 139:13–14).

We are much longed-for: "From your mother's womb I have called you and you are mine." God wants us, and claims us when we are most helpless. Too often we may think only the greats like Jeremiah or Paul are called from the womb. The ordinary ones of us, however, are just as precious in God's sight.

God's womb-compassion can never forget us (annihilate), can never be without tenderness for the child of her womb (abandon). God has carved us on the palms of his hands, has embedded us in the womb of her faithful love (Isaiah 49:15–16). Jesus too has come from the womb of God: "The one who is closest to the Father's heart, he has made God known" (John 1:18).

> Create a safe, inner space for your small and lonely self to retreat to if and when the pain, sadness, rage, terror, and/or mess threatens to overwhelm you.
>
> You may choose a memory from nature, a soft and sensual vacation spot: a warm, sandy beach; a field of wild flowers; a brook hidden among the pines; or a road leading nowhere but laden with the shapes, sounds, and fragrances of creation. You may select a memory of a relationship, expressed with warmth: eyes searching yours, ear bent to listen; a shoulder, breast, or chest in which to bury your face; or the solidity of two hands grasping your shoulders or an arm slung around them. You may create an image of God's womb in which you are lulled gently, the beat of God's heart and rhythm of God's breath reassuring you: you are wanted, a much longed-for child of God.
>
> Go there now. Look, listen, touch, and smell so that you get used to your safe place.

4

The Feeling Heart

In this chapter we will examine some of the ways that we can move from a frozen heart to a feeling heart. Just as when we suffer from frostbite or hypothermia the healing and restoration must be gentle and gradual, so the movement of the heart's healing is also gentle and gradual. We ask the Spirit to come and melt those frozen places with warmth. As the frozen places thaw, the pain and tingling of newly restored feeling may make us yearn for the familiar numbness of cold, the inviting drowsiness of the sleep which precedes death when one has been exposed to freezing temperatures.

In Mark's gospel (Mark 1:40–42) a leper pleads with Jesus, "If you want to, you can cure me." Jesus, feeling sympathy, insists, "Of course I want to." Do we dare to make the leper's prayer our own? And more, do we *want* to be healed? We realize that a cure which restores circulation and feeling to deadened hearts may cause us to wince with new awareness. Since cutting off feelings was a way to survive for children who were deprived of a holding-environment and/or who experienced rejection very early, we need a gentle thawing of that freeze. The Spirit is at work deep within our bodies, in our hearts. Some body exercises of awareness and positive imagery can be a first step to feeling the Spirit's warmth.

> The next time you shower, focus on the experience of what it feels like to have warm or hot water coursing over your body. Let yourself enjoy the warmth and the gentle pressure of the water kneading tired, knotted muscles. Feel the gentle cleansing and the beginnings of newness and energy. Let yourself savor the experience and dare to trust that God meets you in this simple joy and awareness.

Learning to Know a New God

A basic life script which tells us: "There is something radically wrong with me; I do not have any right to exist," requires a cautious approach to life and persons—even to God. Certainly adults who have been physically, sexually, or psychologically abused in their troubled families of origin are not apt to feel naturally at ease with images of God as a parent. For those who have been abused by an older brother or a stronger companion, even the image of Jesus as brother or companion may need reworking. If parents or others in the child's space have failed to live up to the child's trust, it is hard to relate to God who is imaged even as a nurturing adult. The powerless child has been held captive in a chaotic and abusive situation. She has often prayed for God to rescue her, to keep Mommy and Daddy from fighting, to keep Daddy/Mommy from drinking. God has failed. Or at least images and expectations of God have failed.

One woman reveals a memory of praying fervently for her alcoholic father to change. "I had the experience as a child of saying to my mother that I had prayed to God that Daddy stop drinking, but he didn't. Why? Her response was that I had not prayed hard enough. For me, it was not that God had failed, but that—once again—I had failed."

The Jewish scriptures have given us countless images of God other than parent or even nurturing adult. Rock, dew, shield, lamp, fountain of life, light, and fortress are just a few. Hindus have one thousand names for God; Moslems recite one hundred names for God. Images are usually visual, but you might explore some auditory images of God, even some smells and tastes. "Taste and see that the Lord is good."

> Just how does God taste to you?
> What sounds in nature remind you of God?
> What musical instrument is God like?
> What kind of music is God like?
> What color is God?

Some may balk at such imaging of God, claiming that it trivializes God. If a rock was a place of shade and safety for an Israelite in the desert and Israel called God its rock, why cannot God's refreshing action today be described: God is like ice cream sliding down my throat on a blistering hot day?

A young woman who had been profoundly abused, actually tortured, by her father was searching for a way to connect with a God who her father said "willed" her pain. God as father was cruel and terrifying. This woman as an adult learned to express herself through art, finding some peace and joy in her creativity. When she heard that St. Augustine had named God *Beauty* ("O Beauty, ever ancient, ever new, late have I loved you!") she began to cry. Her relief at finding a new name for God and her identification with Augustine gave her so much hope for healing.

Now that we have offered some new possibilities for imaging God, take some time for a "bubble up prayer." Jesus promised us that "fountains of living water" would well up from deep within us (John 7:38). Let the Spirit, your imagination, and your intuition flow freely, without censorship. Let names for, colors of, images of, tastes and smells of, and sounds of God "bubble up" to consciousness.

At other times you might want to write these images. You might finger paint them or express God in your own unique way. You might, for example, dance God. God is so much more than we can express and is forever revealing who God is for us that we can return to this exercise often.

Learning to Feel a New Self

Becoming more aware of the life in and around us can become a means of gently thawing those painful places in the frozen heart. Becoming aware of our own bodily sensations—breathing, sneezing, tasting, smelling, standing barefoot on the grass—lead us to feeling and eventually to God. Sexual experience which expresses love and opens us to mystery can be a privileged place to experience God. There is no bodily sensation or function which cannot be a place where God touches and caresses us with the vitality of being human.

According to Julian of Norwich, the thirteenth century spiritual theologian, no bodily function is too base for God to love us in, even our toilet needs:

Food is shut in within our bodies as in a very beautiful purse. When necessity calls, the purse opens and then shuts again, in the most fitting way. And it is God who does this because I was shown that the goodness of God permeates us even in our humblest need. God does not

> *despise creation, nor does God disdain to serve us in the*
> *simplest function that belongs to our bodies in nature*
> *(p. 28).*

A word of caution, however. For any of us who bear these frozen places, to sense, to feel, even to breathe deeply and steadily, can be such a new experience that it generates feelings of uneasiness. We need not push ourselves to awareness, nor strain to get it right. Again, ask the Spirit to let you experience only what you are ready for right at this moment.

Sometimes focusing on nature is safer than focusing too closely on our own being and bodily processes.

> Treat yourself to whatever in nature is available and
> attractive to you. If you love trees, take some time
> just to look at, smell, and touch your favorite tree. If
> you love the beach, the country, or the mountains,
> and it is feasible to treat yourself to a trip there, do
> it. Even in the most bitter cold the warmth of the sun
> reflecting off the water or snow can be healing. If
> you have a pet which loves to be petted, let that ani-
> mal, its warmth and affection, be a place where God
> can meet you and heal you.

As the frozen places in our hearts begin to thaw we will probably experience the pain of loss for what might have been. Some of the healing for adults who grew up in troubled, dysfunctional families happens when we grieve, mourning the childhood we never had, or the ways in which it was not enough, or not good enough.

With the thaw of awareness the pain of restored feeling can stab deeply. But we have a light within us which thaws in a gentle way, with a tender respect for what we can bear right now. "Light shines in the darkness, and the darkness is not able to suppress it" (John 1:5). This light is Jesus, light of the world and also the light embedded deep within each of us.

Let us ponder just how much light has been seeping into even the most deprived and distorted lives. Have you, in your collection of photographs, one of you as a child which is sad? Go to a place where you can be alone and uninterrupted and contemplate it. Address that child who is the sorrowful, lonely you. Let the child speak to you. Memories will rise, and hopefully so will feelings. Painful feelings. Express them. It may be a lump in your throat. You may cry softly, gently. You may sob. Wail. Rage. Even a trickle of expression will tell you, you *are* alive.

Darkness, loneliness, and sadness were not able to suppress you. You are surviving. With feeling coming even a bit unstuck, you are on the way to life. Mourning our lost childhood, going through the pain of loss, through denial to anger to grief to acceptance, is the way our heart is healed.

Of course God has been healing us even as the holes were gouged out. Even if we were not christened as infants, still there was no blocking God's action in our newborn lives. Many of us were, however, baptized at two weeks or two months of age. A candle was almost as central that day as the baptismal water. The light who is Christ was given to us. More accurately, we were given to him—in this public celebration.

If you have photos of your own christening, or if your church baptizes babies or youngsters and you can participate soon in a family or church's baptismal service, contemplate the child, the candle, and Christ at work in that child's heart. To contemplate means to look deeply, to notice, to allow feelings and desires to arise. It means responding to what you see, to what you remember, to what you imagine, and to what you want. Can you "see" the risen Christ with that child? What does Christ do? want? feel? Now *you* be that child; see yourself as that infant and let Christ do for you, want for you, and feel for you.

Letting God Reparent the Child Within

We cannot go back and redo our chronological childhood. It is possible, however, to invite God to touch and heal some of those hurts which happened very early in our lives, even before we had words to think about what happened. Some pain and deprivation began earlier than our verbal memory. Our earliest need is to be held and to have our basic needs understood and responded to. Our earliest "dance" as infants is the ballet of molding contentedly to the shape of our mothering figure when we are graciously held, or stiffening in distress when our needs are not met.

In this next exercise, we invite you to image yourself a newborn infant. Ask the Spirit to let you experience the empathy of God who understands, before you even have words, who you are and what you need. Whatever your pain of being abused, neglected, rejected, used, or abandoned, try to let yourself be held by the God who yearns for your whole-ing. At first this exercise may seem too foreign to your own experience, too painful. Just read it through quickly. You may prefer to imagine another baby—or may choose never to "get into" this exercise. Good enough. God has myriad ways to heal your infant heart.

> Picture yourself as a newborn infant. Your tiny mouth is sucking involuntarily. Your eyes are shut. Your wee fingers are curled into a little fist. Let your feeling-memory experience the comfort of being nestled contentedly in arms which gather you to the comfort of a breast or a lap. Someone holds you who delights in your very being. God. You are curled into God's body, molded into God. You are close enough to hear again the reassuring heartbeat rhythm which comforted you in the womb. Let yourself breathe

quietly and comfortably, listening, feeling the pulse of God, smelling—no words. Stay with these pre-verbal sensations and the emotions which accompany them for as long as you remain comfortable.

If you open the eyes of your infant self, you see God looking at you tenderly and with great love. How do you feel? Is it difficult to hold God's eyes with your own? Do you feel shy? sleepy? reassured? frightened? loved? ashamed to be seen? If you can keep gazing at God (or some prefer to use the image of a more concretely human Jesus or Mary), see if you can absorb some of God's delight in you. See your beauty mirrored in God's eyes. If you start to sleep or need to close your eyes against so much unconditional love, do so. God will hold you close for as long as you need. Just enjoy the total body sensation of molding with God's body.

One of the legacies of not getting what we needed as infants is the feeling of helplessness which surrounds some of our pain as adults. We feel helpless about our fears or feelings of shame or depression. The helplessness which makes an infant so appealing and dear becomes a psychological prison when we become adult. Very often the only thing we can do with our helplessness is admit it and surrender it. This is the first step of the twelve-step recovery process for addictions. Admitting our powerlessness can be used with any psychological distress which feels unmanageable to us.

Our reparenting God, like the good-enough mother, is drawn to our helplessness and longs to respond to us. "Oh, if only you would open your mouth! How I long to feed you" of Psalm 81 might be rephrased here: Oh, if only you would let me hold you, carry you, caress you, admire you, love you! How I long to melt you into myself, mold you into my heart!

> Take a little time to hold however you feel helpless before God. Show God your neediness. Open your hands on your lap. Let your open hands be body-prayer for your desire to let God's healing warm the frozen places inside you.

This open-handed, open-hearted prayer needs to be repeated frequently because God does not ordinarily heal quickly, all at once. It might become a daily prayer to trust the warmth of God's "holding environment," to trust that God is not ashamed of our helplessness and, in fact, is drawn to our neediness by God's own womb-compassion.

"Look at Jesus looking at you, humbly and tenderly," instructs St. Teresa of Avila. That is contemplation. We need not go into a life of solitude to practice such simple contemplation, if occasionally we can stop to look. While waiting for Sunday worship to begin, while showering, or while snatching that first cup of coffee alone before the bustle begins, look at Jesus looking at you.

Humbly. Jesus who is "humble of heart" looks at us humbly. The root of this English word is the Latin *humus*—earth, ground, dirt. Human, humility, and humor all share this Latin root. Jesus looks at us *as* human, understanding in his very body—brain, nerve cells, and memory traces—how it is for us, as it was for him, to be frail, weak, vulnerable, tired, limited. Jesus looks at us with humility, in awe at our common creaturehood, marveling at the truth of who we are, so naked and defenseless. Jesus looks at us with humor, delight, and joy, "that my joy in you may be complete" (John 15:11). Jesus rejoices in us just as we are.

Tenderly. Jesus attends to us and tends us. Tenderly comes from a Latin root which means a stretching, and he stretches toward us. He first attends, pays attention, and notices our holes, scabs, and scars. He listens and turns toward us. He tends us and binds up our wounds with tenderness. He has put a body on the action of God, so uniquely attuned to our various situations and needs:

The lost I will look for, the straying I will bring back, the injured I will bandage, the sick I will heal, and the strong and healthy I will set out to play. —Ezekiel 34:16

Parents look at their newborns, hopefully with awe and tenderness. Parents mirror for us as infants. What we see of ourselves in their eyes has a profound impact on how we view ourselves throughout life. Did we find hatred or anxiety, joy or tranquility? Jesus can remirror for us now as adults. "Look at Jesus looking at you, humbly and tenderly." Invite Jesus to be your parenting figure. You are the twinkle in his eye.

Imagine yourself as newborn (a photo of yourself or a more recent memory of a newborn may spark you). God places you in Jesus' arms. It is the first time Jesus has ever held you. Look up into Jesus' eyes. What do you see there? What feeling is shining through? How are you feeling as he looks at you? Let your whole body, right now, reflect that feeling in you. Stay with your body and its feeling(s) for as long as you can. Stop here for a while . . .

If your body is relaxed and the feelings are pleasant, just enjoy. If your body is tense and rigid, if you feel afraid or angry, tell Jesus how you are feeling. You do not insult him; he looks at you humbly. He wants to know how you are hurting; he looks at you tenderly.

We know people who have done this exercise almost daily for years; we know others who try periodically but find it too painful or too frightening. Jesus goes at our pace. If you do return to it, let newborn-you grow up day by day, month by month. Let Jesus grow you up. Jesus will reparent you. As Julian of Norwich writes: "God feels great delight to be our Father and God feels great delight to be our Mother" (p. 85). She adds, even about the male, Jesus: "And Jesus is our true Mother in whom we are endlessly carried" (p. 99).

Jesus and the Frozen Heart

In this section we will flesh out a gospel story in the hope that you too will feel free to use the good news imaginatively and creatively. Scripture does what it says. The word of God will reshape us imaginatively and creatively too.

The following gospel passage about the Gerasene demoniac is a stark and dramatic one. It was chosen because too many children from dysfunctional families grow up with such a profound sense of shame, feeling as though they do not have a right not only to belong but even to exist. Unlike the Gerasene man possessed by demons, we often function well enough and with competence which ranges from adequate to gifted. Inside, however, the feelings of shame and negative self-image are like sharp stones with which we gouge ourselves. The wounds may be hidden but they are real. If you need to "run away" from this story, know that God respects where you are and meets you there. God goes at our pace. With God, a return to the womb is not cowardice. It is grace-space, a place to wait until we are ready.

Jesus is attracted to outcasts.

The wind and sea have just obeyed an exhausted Jesus, roused from sleep on board a boat by his fearful friends. So it must be that Jesus wants to land in this lonely spot on a foreign shore, the territory of the Gerasenes (Mark 5:1–20). The boat is beached, Peter holding it steady offering Jesus a hand as he hops to the sand. The disciples hold back, puzzled, but Jesus' eyes roam up and down the beach;

he squints as he stoops and peers into some caves used as tombs. There is a stench.

Suddenly, they hear a roar and a clanging. Springing into daylight, dragging a heavy chain, a skeleton of a man with a filthy beard, ragged hair and wounds festering on his naked body, rushes toward Jesus. Peter's fist clenches; he is ready for action.

As the man runs, a shackle still attached to his limping leg, he gashes his chest with a sharp rock. Fresh blood flows. His screams convey both fear and fierceness. As Peter moves forward to defend Jesus, Jesus stands his ground, with concern etched on his face but peace in his body. The man drops to the sand. "Jesus!" he cries. "Jesus!" he sobs. "Jesus!" he wails. "Why have you come here? Go away. I am insane. I am dangerous. I am out of control. I smell. I am ugly, mean. I am full of hatred. In God's name, go away. Do not torment me. Stop looking at me. Go away!"

Jesus, meanwhile, has dropped on one knee to the sand and softly touches the man's lice-ridden hair. He speaks with power coursing through his whole body, "Unclean spirit, come out of this man." Their two voices crash together in the wind: Jesus' voice crackling with anger and authority, the man's with rage and terror. Jesus' power prevails.

About two thousand pigs were lost that day. The townsfolk clamber over the rocks, unaware now of the tombs' odor, their eyes fixed on two men sitting close together on the beach. As a fire burns, a cup is shared by the two, their heads bent close together. To one side, huddled close to the Jewish boat, is a group of men who also look on in bewilderment. No one can overhear Jesus and the man as the crowd from town watches at a distance.

Jesus has warmed a wet cloth and is daubing the man's new wound. "Can you tell me about it? Tell me about your isolation out here?"

"I hated myself, Jesus. I knew I was a failure, a nothing. I knew it since I was a child, a disappointment to my family, a butt of ridicule to the boys in town. I began to cut myself when the others would make fun of me. I got some relief from the shame of it. I could hurt myself more than they could. Gradually I got more public in my wild lashings out. The town council banished me—but I would sneak back to my family, undress and gash myself in front of them. They had me chained to the rocks out here, would bring me food and water, try to keep me clothed. I enjoyed ripping off my clothes in front of them—they were so very proper. They ripped my self-respect from me so I returned in kind."

Jesus has stopped washing the wound; he is focused only on the man's face. His eyes close and pain creases his face.

That man is you . . .
Jesus speaks to your heart, and says . . .
You respond . . .

5

The Receptive Heart

In this chapter we will examine the slow, sometimes imperceptible movement as the hungry heart opens and gradually becomes receptive instead of grasping. In the previous chapter, the "bubble up" prayer may have provided a taste of receiving, not from the outside, but from within ourselves. Deep in our unconscious, the Spirit, God's "love poured out into our hearts" (Romans 5:5), comes to the help of our weakness. Deep within where so much is buried—feelings, memories, images, hungers, hopes—the Spirit is "putting our inarticulate groanings into words which God can understand" (Romans 8:26). So much of who we are is unutterable and inarticulate; we do not have the words; the memories and feelings are pre-verbal, the time before our infant self had words to describe them. Terror, grief, and rage, so central to an infant's healthy emotional makeup, may have been choked off. We are anxious (*angostos,* choked) and inarticulate.

Learning to Know a New Self

The Spirit will reveal to us who we are. What we must first receive is our true self, one named and claimed by God. Throughout scripture, God gives new names. God's naming us now may heal some labels which have crippled us. If we have needed new images of God, we probably also need new images of ourselves. A hundred names for our own self? Or is there just one which has haunted us and hollowed out the emptiness of our heart even more deeply?

Brad is a burly law enforcement officer who battled into middle age with a father who taunted him and insulted him as a child with vulgar names. On retreat, he blurted out to his retreat director in amazement, relief, and joy: "God knows my name! And it isn't asshole!"

Linda's mother called her a slut even before she had started school. She grew up frightened that her mother's name for her had defined her forever. To ward off acting out her label, she joined a community of women religious right after high school. Still the terror that her mother *really* knew her, knew something about her which she did not know, lurked.

One day, during a Holy Week retreat, Sister Linda was praying with the account of Jesus' passion. In her imagination he was dragging his cross along the narrow streets of Jerusalem. His dear friend John kept popping over the heads of the crowds as he would push and jump and try to run along so as to keep up with Jesus. "Jesus," he called out, in Linda's prayer, "Jesus, why are you doing this? Tell them you give up, you'll go home and keep quiet!"

Jesus could barely turn his head to catch his friend's eye. With great weariness he muttered, "Oh, John, don't *you* understand?" Linda was fascinated as the gospel characters took on such life in her prayer.

"Let's go home. Why are you doing this?" John repeated.

"I'm doing this for Linda," Jesus replied.

To Linda's horror, out of John's mouth hurtled the name her mother had branded her with. Over the heads of the crowds, his face twisted with disgust, John cried, "For that slut?!"

Jesus stopped. Painfully he stood up straight, found his friend's eye, and said proudly: "She's no slut! She's mine!"

On that day Sister Linda's heart began to heal. "This one shall write on his hand (on her heart), 'The Lord's own' " (Isaiah 44:5).

One adult whose family life was quite unstable remembers how her grandmother's home was a steadying place for her. Her memory, a learning by heart, was of her grandmother's opening wide her arms, her face just as open and welcoming, as she called out, "My darling!"

> Have you a memory of someone so eager and happy to receive you—as an adult now? What did/do they call you? How did they come to name you? Rest in and enjoy and learn by heart.

> By what name does God call you? "God's darling grew fat and frisky," scripture assures the hungry heart (Deuteronomy 32:15). "Fear not, my people, my _____ (insert your name), my darling, whom I have chosen" (Isaiah 44:2).

> As once you let bubble up some images of God from deep within you where the Spirit prays and plays, now ask the Spirit to teach you what images and names God has for you. Do not think. Just wait quietly to feel and intuit what bubbles up.

Learning to Receive a New Self

Sometimes it is hard to believe that our greatest gift from God is our very life and being. "We are truly God's work of art" (Ephesians 2:10). Too often, those of us with hungry hearts grow up knowing more about de-selfing than about a legitimate solid sense of self. De-selfing is the word by which therapist Harriet Lerner describes the behaviors and ways of being which adults use to deny or distract from their own legitimate needs. The seeds for de-selfing have been sown early in life when a baby whose mothering is not good enough learns to contract against its own needs and neediness.

Legitimate needs are not to be equated with the greedy "me-first" attitude which has been a characteristic of recent times, fueled by the advertising industry's creation of artificial needs and wants. De-selfing springs rather from the hidden, denied neediness of the person who did not get enough physical, emotional, and spiritual nourishment at some critical moments of early development. The de-selfer thus grows up with an insatiable hunger for others, a vulnerability, a dependency which does not reverence the human reality of separateness and the need for self-care. Boundaries of what one can legitimately be for another, or do for another, get blurred.

In recent decades the notion of co-dependence has received increasing attention in the field of the study of addictions. Co-dependence has been called the prevailing form of illness in a dysfunctional family system. Melody Beattie's definition describes the co-dependent as a person "who has let another person's behavior affect him or her, and who is obsessed with controlling that person's behavior (p. 28)." The co-dependent person is one who de-selfs so as not to lose the other on whom life centers. Co-dependents are addicted to relationships.

The co-dependent adult who has grown up with a dysfunctional family of origin, with either boundaries which mesh and meld or walls which distance and defend, has to guess at what normal relating looks like. Where to say yes and where to say no to the needs, wants, and hungers of others become painful questions for the de-selfing adult. Sometimes such a person gives and gives until he or she drops. Only illness gives him or her permission to refuse requests for time, attention, money, listening, favors, and so on.

One who is so hungry for care, or so afraid to stop giving lest he or she be forgotten, needs to acknowledge the self, damaged and needy though it be. "Listen to me, Lord, poor and needy as I am" (Psalm 86:1).

> Take some time to share with God (or Jesus or Spirit) just where, when, and with whom you feel drained, empty, and unsure about boundaries.

We need the Spirit of light to help us discern boundaries, needs, and real responsibilities from our duty-bound, compulsive caretaking. This is an area in which we can become blinded and confused. Our efforts and striving to care for others, or even to right the injustices of the world, can assume a driven quality which may temporarily make us feel good, but which can lead to exhaustion and burnout. When the Spirit, rather than our compulsive false self leads us to love and justice, we receive that love and justice first as God's gifts to us. If they are truly God's gifts, we are gradually freed from righteousness and patronizing contempt for those whom we serve.

> Take some time to ask God to fill and refresh you. Imagine a brook, stream, or river and place yourself beside it. See, hear, and smell that running water. Then pray from Psalm 23.

> *In meadows of green grass God lets me lie. To restful waters God leads me to revive my drooping spirit. God spreads a banquet before me.*   —Psalm 23

What do you want God to spread before you? Name your banquet items—and they need not be actual foods—for God. See your servant-God ministering to you, giving you what you need and hunger for. Then just rest.

Some of us identify with the elder son in the parable of the prodigal son and welcoming father. We have worked so hard and asked for so little for ourselves. Reimage the scene after reading slowly, preferably out loud, the passage from Luke 15:11–32. Tell God your complaint, voice your disapproval, and show God how deprived you are feeling. Then hear, with as open a heart as you can, inserting your own name: "My _____, all I have is yours."

Remembering and Being Filled

Remember in vivid detail and then savor one life experience which has been a source of life and vitality for you. Think of some moment or experience in your life which did once nourish you.

Remembering, as specifically as possible, thus becomes a way to be filled and refreshed again. As the memory returns to you in concrete detail, enjoy what you see, hear, and feel.

Mary, a middle-aged woman whose family was crippled by premature death, shares the following story, one moment in her life which continues to energize her and give her hope. Mary's mother died shortly after her birth as a result of complications from pregnancy. Although no one ever blamed her for her mother's death in any overt way, she blamed herself. As a little girl she had been told by her aunt never to talk about her mother because it made her daddy feel sad. The weight of this taboo in her child's mind evolved into a sense of guilt and responsibility for her mother's death. She carried this weight for many years, even long after her father had died. She often used to think how much better it would have been for everyone if she instead of her mother had died.

One day, long after she had grown into the successful professional woman she is, she was visiting her aunt and uncle. They were reminiscing about what a wonderful person her mother had been and how sad that she died when she did. Uncharacteristically, Mary blurted out to her uncle what she had thought secretly for so many years: "It's too bad that she died instead of me." Her uncle, a beefy Irishman who ordinarily was very undemonstrative with his feelings, came over to her and put both hands on Mary's shoulders. He looked into her eyes with the greatest tenderness and said," But we have *you*. Don't you understand that? We have you." The tenderness and conviction of this dear man who had become like a second father to Mary somehow healed her painful place of self-blame. When Mary remembers his kind face, looking at her with both a perplexity that she should even have such a self-doubt and an unabashed delight in her being, she is refreshed again.

> Take some time now to let yet another memory, perhaps like Mary's, bubble up for you. A word, a smile, the feeling of being loved, anything which nourishes you. Pay attention to how you feel as you remember.

When we remember in this way we are literally re-membering, taking back into ourselves something which can fill our hungers and give us life and energy again. When the memory is an affirming, positive one, and if we let ourselves re-experience it in a relaxed and gentle way, it continues to have the power to heal and make our hearts more whole.

But what about painful memories? How do we remember and rework these events and the feelings attached to them, in ways which can bring wholeness? How do we re-member those happenings in our lives which took place at so young an age, before we could even think in words, let alone speak? These pre-verbal memories are powerful feeling traces inside our bodies—yearnings, flinchings, terrors, and trembles.

Because of the magnificent human thrust toward survival, we learn early on to defend ourselves from that which is too painful to bear. In instances of physical and sexual abuse, young children sometimes literally seal off painful pieces into separate personalities. Others may repress agonizing memories which remain totally unavailable, perhaps for a lifetime or until something or someone jogs the memory back into excruciatingly painful focus.

Made public in the papers and on "Nightline," the sexual aberration of American University's president splashed into headlines some years ago. This brilliant, driven man's story is too typical of many adult children of dysfunctional families. A workaholic who regularly put in one hundred hours a week, he had successfully sealed off some early memories of sexual and emotional abuse until his father's funeral tore away a bandage of defense. He was left vulnerable to a compulsive sexual behavior which cost him his brilliant academic career. This scholar of astronomy and accomplished administrator said in one of his first public interviews: "I could understand a quasar 15 billion light years away, but I couldn't understand the boy that's now within the man" (*Washington Post,* June 7, 1990, p. D–1). On the surface it appears that the cost of all this is the stellar career of an extraordinarily gifted human being who transformed a university. But the real cost is the life of the child, the adult child who literally got worked to death in the process of trying to contain pain.

The re-membering of agonizing experiences can be a very shattering experience, best done with a competent and compassionate companion, therapist, or spiritual director. Inviting Jesus or the God we trust into painful memories can be healing and wholing. With the Spirit of truth leading us into memories, we can go at our own pace. To re-member and re-feel and re-work some of the abusive events of infancy and childhood can free us for new, creative, and more genuine attitudes, feelings, and behaviors in the present. We need not remain prisoners of childhood, the original title of Alice Miller's little classic, when we have a God who wants to set us free in the open, who is strong to save.

Letting God Reparent Us

She is very little, twelve to fourteen months old. She has been playing on the sand a few feet from her mother, totally absorbed. Yet every few minutes she glances back at Mummy who is sitting nearby. Suddenly she scoots back to Mummy, grabs her hand, and tugs. Together they start toward the ocean. The water sparkles with ten thousand sun diamonds and the baby's eyes gleam with excitement at this wide, wonderful new world. She tugs at Mummy again. She is squealing with delight and, firmly steadied by Mummy's grasp, is running on tiptoe with confidence and eagerness toward the water, looking around at anyone whose eye she can meet, but regularly checking up to catch Mummy's glance. The little girl is held by that glance as steadily as by her mother's hand.

This moving away from the mother and yet being held by either a glance or a hand is typical of a baby this age. Mother lets her go to explore and play, but is also there to steady and refuel her.

> Take a little time to *be* that child, the eager, exploring, delighted little person who is learning to trust, discovering that the world is inviting and basically trustworthy. When you get tired or overwhelmed go back to God and rest—"like a weaned child on its mother's lap (Psalm 131)."

God, in loving foolishness, lets us "use" God's steady, good-mothering presence. If, as toddlers, our own mothering was inconsistent and not filling enough, there are ways in which our grown-up selves still mimic the little exploring conqueror of the universe who we were at one year of age. Busy about all our many projects, as adults we just glance back occasionally during the day at the God who is steadily growing us up.

> Take some time to glance at God now, to be reassured, to let yourself be nourished and filled and steadied by God's glance.

The prophet Hosea describes God as teaching us (Israel/Ephraim) to move off the lap to explore, to play with utter confidence in God's steadying nearness.

> *When Israel was a child I loved that child. . . . It was I who taught Ephraim to walk, who took them in my arms; I drew them with leading strings, with bonds of love; bent down to nourish them and lifted them like an infant to the cheek. . . . I stooped to feed my child.* —Hosea 11:1–4

> Rest with this passage, substituting your own name in place of "Israel" and "Ephraim." Let your self be nourished by this word of God, by God's own consistent kindness.

Jesus and the Hungry Heart

Jesus is no stranger to the hungers of our hearts, those empty, lacking spaces. He knows in his own skin and through his being with the persons whose lives he touched, all about hurt and loneliness. He understands being caught in rigid religious systems which fasten more burdens than they loosen. He knows about hunger, both physical and emotional.

It is almost impossible to find a gospel story in which Jesus is not feeding the hungers of the human heart or slaking real or metaphorical thirst.

> Let yourself travel around Galilee with him as you take time right now to remember some favorite gospel scenes. Notice what you see and hear. Who is with Jesus? How is Jesus with the person(s)?

As mentioned earlier, Jesus is the best image of God, the human expression of God's passionate desire to set us free, fill our hungers, and liberate us from the addictions to which our hungry hearts cling.

Jesus could have chosen all sorts of ways to help us remember that he lives with us and continues to act through us. He chose, however, to be remembered in bread, broken and shared. If we examine the earliest gospel, the gospel of Mark written closest to the historical life of Jesus, we notice the verbs which describe Jesus' doing and being: listening, being moved with pity, touching, forgiving, and teaching. Mark's gospel gives us the earliest version of the feeding of the crowds. Let us imagine what it would be like to be part of the crowd which hungrily followed this man Jesus. We already know what it was like for Jesus. Mark tells us how Jesus felt when he saw all those who had assembled: "He pitied them, for they were like sheep without a shepherd" (Mark 6:34). Let us now put on the heart and flesh of one of the people of Galilee, leading a life marked by the daily ordinariness at that time, in some ways not so different from our own.

Jesus is attracted to the hungry.

> *She twists her body so her leg will not fall asleep. Her mind drifts from his sermon for a moment, distracted by a rumble from her stomach. "How do I stretch my food-buying money?"*

Her heart snaps back to him. "Who is this man who seems to understand so well the nooks and crannies of my heart? He speaks to me so deeply, yet in concrete stories which I can understand. I am only one woman in this crowd, hungry, tired. I am so puzzled by these Pharisees, by their religious system which is becoming more and more burdensome in its strict requirements."

Her thoughts wander off to remember a story going around about Jesus: "Why, only last month this Jesus was walking along on the sabbath and his hungry friends started eating the grain along the side of the road. When the Pharisees challenged this, Jesus actually stood up to them and said: 'The sabbath was made for human beings; we were not made for the sabbath!' Who is this Jesus who is so human and compassionate about real human hunger?"

As she ponders in her heart, her stomach reminds her again: "I left home with hardly any food. Now I've lost track of time and place in my curiosity to spend more time with this fellow. Hah! My stomach knows that it's been ten hours now and I know we're very far away from town. Oh well, hunger is not a new thing for me. Being so completely understood, that is new to me—and hearing my heart read back to me!"

There is some commotion around Jesus. He has stopped speaking. She wants to voice her wonder out loud. She whispers to the woman on her left: "You know, I was sitting near the edge of the crowd while he was talking earlier today, and he caught my eye. For a minute our eyes locked and it was like being known and loved and filled. It was as though all those stories I heard about his healing and forgiving got locked into that one look. I feel brand new.

"But wait—where did this bread come from? It's a bigger, much more fresh and moist piece than the old crust which I had left when he asked us to pool our food a few minutes ago." Now her wonder silences her, and she muses: "It's the oddest thing. Am I going crazy? This bread tastes just like that look he gave me."

Now it is later that year. She wants to celebrate Passover in Jerusalem. It has taken all her savings and all her energy to travel from Galilee. She is hoping to glimpse Jesus at the feast.

She does not notice who is at the center of the crowd in the adjacent court as she finds the box designated for alms for the poor. He notices her. "See that poor widow, putting in two small coins. I tell you, she put in more than all the rest. The others gave from their extra money, but she put in all that she had to live on" (Luke 21:1–4).

His steady gaze suddenly catches her attention. She blushes and looks down. "And you," his smile says across the courtyard, "You fill me, dear woman, because what you give to the least, you are giving to me." Once again, his smile tastes like the finest bread.

That widow is you, and you say to Jesus . . .
and you feel . . .
Jesus responds to you . . .

6

The Simple Heart

In this chapter we will sketch some suggestions for prayer which may help us become more comfortable with our "true self," the ragged edges of our humanness. In this discovery and celebration of our own true, separate selves with both the beauty and vulnerability of being human, we discover also the capacity to enjoy and value others as separate persons with their own longings and limits.

We learn to come home to ourselves, to others, and to the realities of those parts of our world which we cannot change. In that process our hungry need for approval from the outside can lessen. As we let go of our own needs to be perfect, our irritation that others do not always notice and applaud these efforts diminishes and fades into a greater comfortableness with ourselves and others.

We may even discover to our wonderment that we require less power and pizzazz from God, and that we can accept God's own beauty and vulnerability. As God surprises us with the many facets of our own true self, we can dare to look at and love the many faces of our God.

Learning to Know a New God—Again

In an earlier chapter we offered some possibilities for images of God—colors, tastes, music—which were founded on sensations of beauty and mystery rather than on a specifically personal image. Yet we concluded the chapter with our infant selves nestled and molded against a God who was imaged as a kind, accepting, nurturing mother-figure.

Scripture does image God as both father and mother, as well as shepherd carrying the lamb at his breast, as seamstress making us leather garments, as potter shaping the clay of us, and as nursemaid giving suckle to a baby. While God as champion might console us when we need a protector, images of God as warrior, king, judge, or lion are more likely to frighten and distance us, especially if adult authorities once terrorized or brutalized us. God's anger, sometimes punishing anger, is a reality in scripture; God's jealousy, grief, and hatred are also described. As our own sensations and feelings become thawed and begin to flow freely, God may invite us to pay attention to God's feelings, deep and long-lasting emotions which medieval theologian St. Thomas Aquinas called passions. As our own hungers are filled, God may ask us to appreciate God's own hungers, the desires of God's heart, that passion which means a deep, intense, focused desire.

The most frequently named passions of God's heart are love and faithful devotion, *hesed* and *'emet*. Those emotions and God's womb-compassion, delight, joy, and exuberance (Zephaniah 3:17–18) are such a comfort. Sometimes we want to use that old "splitting" defense, however, and keep God in a plastic pose of kindness, not allowing God the full range and depth of passion which we experience. The more anyone comes close to us, however, the more we will discover his or her true self, a self which is ambiguous, a blend of good and bad, a personality not pastel but multicolored with deep rich colors.

Sometimes religion has "split" in order to keep God distant, plastic, and pastel; preachers have named what is evil and assigned it all to the devil. God tried to overcome the split in Jesus who put flesh on God's heart, and God's passions. In Jesus, God has come very close, very real, and very human. "To see me, Philip, is to have seen the Father" (John 14:9). Jesus, like us in all things, could well have asked Mary, Joseph, and God:

> *What would have happened if I had appeared before you,*
> *bad, ugly, angry, jealous, lazy, dirty, smelly? . . . And I*
> *was all of these things as well. . . .* —Miller, p. 15

What *would* have happened? Jesus is "like us in everything . . . but sin" (Hebrews 2:17; 4:15). But "bad" is not necessarily sin in God's eyes. Dirt and unpleasant odors do not offend God. And Jesus did choose to become "unclean," which the Jewish encyclopedia terms "a state of alienation from God," when he touched a leper or a corpse or was touched by a woman with an issue of blood. God and the guardians of religious systems often see sin differently.

Sometimes all anger has been called sin, instead of the good and helpful emotion which it is. When we as children experienced anger, even the most just anger, even simply an eyebrow lifted in warning or disapproval, we could be terrified. Parents are so big and powerful, we so small and helpless. Hopefully as we matured, as we developed friendships and love relationships, we learned to give and receive anger appropriately. We learned that anger expressed and worked through can be a sign of trustful intimacy and can lead to even deeper intimacy. Anger need not be violent, punitive, terrorizing, and destructive.

God invites us to reimage God's anger, not as annihilating rage directed at a helpless child, but as an expression of God's self and passionate caring, a call to an adult friend for an even more solid bond. "You Satan," Jesus shouted at his best friend; he then not only did not abandon Peter but kept inviting him into situations of closeness.

We can image a God of deep passions and desires, a God who expresses a true self, not a plastic patsy but a really loving, angry, joyful, protective, jealous, caring, hating, grieving, kind, and faithful God. We can learn a new God by paying close attention to the one who put flesh on God's deep passions and desires, the best image of God, Jesus.

Learning to Enjoy the True Self

"I am who I am" (Exodus 3:14) is the first name God reveals to Moses. Only later does Moses learn that God's name reflects the passions of God's heart: "merciful with womb-compassion, slow to anger, rich in kindness and fidelity" (Exodus 34:6). From our mother's womb we just are. We are who we are. "Naked we came from our mother's womb and naked we return" (Job 1:21). As infants, we are naked sensation, raw emotion, pure need, and indomitable will; yet we do not know how to think.

How quickly we learn to control all that simple being. As we learn to think in more complex ways, we sometimes, in order to please our parents or merely to make it in this computerized society, choke off that half of our brain out of which simple being operates. We create ourselves, in control, and weary ourselves with the frenetic, frantic activity which too often chokes off enjoyment of the simple.

God hopes to heal that frantic, controlled, and controlling heart, but does not abandon us in our refusal to be a true self. We have, most of us, fashioned for ourselves an ideal self, an idol self "with eyes which see not, ears which hear not . . . nor is there a breath of life in them" (Psalm 115:5, 7). Nor can "the hearts of idols understand" (Isaiah 44:18). Cut off from ourselves, somewhat wooden, or perhaps bronze or gold, we too often cannot understand ourselves and so judge ourselves without compassion. Too often it follows that we judge others without understanding and compassion as well.

We create an ideal self who must look good (cosmetic, diet industries) and perform well (college acceptance, million dollar athletes). We tire, managing everyone's impression of us. Life can become one long "photo opportunity." As Isaiah warns, idols "must be borne up on shoulders, carried as burdens by the weary" (Isaiah 46:1). A modern day minister, Merle Jordan in *Taking on the Gods*, challenges pastoral counselors to confront these gods which we tend to create. We can too often trudge along, hiding behind the false self, wooden idol, trying to become that ideal self who has become our god. The glittering image masks the empty heart and wearies us with its demands.

> God invites us to put down our work baskets; God wants to take the heavy burdens off our backs (Psalm 81:7). This is the will, the passionate desire of God. Who or what is in your work basket? Can you image them concretely? Then list your responsibilities: persons, groups, activities, and events. Go over your list, marking who is in charge of each responsibility. Mark your name, perhaps someone else's, maybe God's. If you died tomorrow, who would take over each duty?
>
> Now listen as God speaks directly to you:
>
> *I have carried you from your infancy. Even to your old age I am the same. Even when your hair is gray, it is I who bear you . . . I who will continue and I who will carry you to safety.* —Isaiah 46:3–4
>
> Can you hand over your work basket and your lists to God?

" 'Tis a gift to be simple." The old hymn exhorts: "Turn, turn . . . and you will be in the valley of delight." How to experience simplicity and delight, once the work basket is handed over to God? The heart of the idol has no understanding and so it becomes judgmental: this is bad, this is good; this is right, this is wrong; this is better, this is best, this is perfect. There can be no delight, no freedom, only measuring, only more and more and more.

Mary, the mother of Jesus, offers us a way to "turn, turn" so we can come to the "valley of delight" found at the heart of our true self. Mary ponders everything in her heart, treasures it. It may have been easy to treasure the loud shout of joy from her cousin Elizabeth who welcomed her. It may have been more difficult to receive the promise made through Simeon that a sword of sorrow would pierce her heart. It must have been terrifying, however, even to hear the message of boisterous, smelly, dirty shepherds who burst in on the very young family the night Jesus was born. Luke writes that even this experience, however, Mary treasured in her heart (Luke 2:19).

> Image yourself after some strenuous activity, or worn out by some heavy responsibility. You are exhausted. You find a quiet spot, breathe deeply, feet up, eyes closed.
>
> As the shepherds burst in on Mary, suddenly _____ bursts in upon you. What, deep within you, is that blank? A feeling of jealousy? A sexual impulse? The memory of a stupid decision? A hint of incompetence? Let something within you which you hold in contempt, some trait, sin, or defect of character, come before you. You are limited, weak, and flawed. Try to treasure that in your heart. First, acknowledge the _____. Look at

it and ponder it, without judging. How did this
_____ come to be? Let curiosity replace judg-
ment. This _____ is neither good nor bad;
it just is.

When our hearts can accept our own reality, our creaturehood, our limits and mortality, when we can treasure in our
hearts what seems so base and of the earth in us, on that day we
know from experience that even where sin abounds, grace so
much more abounds. We are who we are. We are not God. This
simple acceptance of our self as we are leads to understanding of
ourselves, forgiveness of ourselves for being human, and eventually the laying side of the idol of the self-ideal which demand-
ed such continual, frantic polishing.

Letting God Reparent Us

How God yearns for us to be simply who we are, no pre-
texts, no need to manipulate or control or try to appear more perfect than we are. "God knows how we are made; God remembers
that we are dust" (Psalm 103).

The child is two and a half years old now, marching tri-
umphantly around the back yard. He spies some bright red tulips
and darts over to examine their shape and smell. In a flash he
picks three or four and races back across the yard, wrapped in a
toddler's secure sense of bringing a treasure to his mother. How
will she receive this gift? Serenely, despite her chagrin at seeing
her garden ravaged? Or will she rage at what she judges to be
baby's destructiveness?

Our God is like the mother who can smile and take delight
in her young son when in the midst of toilet training he got busy
in his play. He forgot and filled his pants. Then he carried *that*
treasure to his mother with the same pride with which he pre-
sented tulips the day before. She received his gift with as much
enthusiasm, oohing and aahing as she had over tulips. God is
like that.

One of the steps in the early process of becoming a separate self is learning to define boundaries by saying no. Those "terrible twos" which in their own way are as turbulent an entrance into selfhood as their later counterpart, adolescence, get some of their definition by the magnificent "no." Dare we believe that our God can love us and accept us even in our "no"? Even in our haughty rages, if we dare to feel, express, and share them? It is hard for any of us who have been required to be or behave a certain way in order to receive approval to risk the approval of God by saying "no." We are not referring to gross sin, conscious refusal of God's love, or conscious injustice to another human being. Our "no" arises in response to the Spirit's nudges, our own best impulses and intuitions. If "no" is our honest response, God does not walk away. Moses, Jeremiah, David, Peter, and the rich young man could all say no, and Jacob could even, momentarily, pin God to the ground.

In order to separate from our mothers, we must keep on saying an occasional "no." When an occasional "no" to God defines the boundaries of our separate self, we are exercising our free will, which most of us would agree is God's greatest gift to us. We are indeed separate from God. To say no is not sin but separateness. We are not God, nor is God under our control. God is utterly free, and separate, and other. "No" signifies all that.

Jesus, according to Luke's gospel, does not ask us always to be perfect, which for many of us means without mistakes or weakness but conforming and compliant. Matthew's gospel urges, be perfect, but Luke changes Matthew's "perfect" to "compassionate." "Be compassionate as your heavenly Father is compassionate" (Luke 6:36). Required to be as close to perfect as possible as youngsters, we may have internalized that demand, made it our own; then we could demand perfection of ourselves and others. Exploited ourselves, we lose touch with our own capacity to exploit. Once controlled by adults, we have learned to control ourselves and try too often to control others.

Take some time to contemplate your own toddler-
hood. If you have any photos, spend some time
looking at the little person you see. How do you feel
about that little one? How does God feel about you
as you trotted about, gathering treasures? Trust
whatever respect and love and delight that you both
can take in this small child who still lives within
you.

Now picture yourself with your two little feet dug
in, your hands on your tiny hips, your jaw thrust
upward, your eyes hard. "No," you say to God, "no
way!" How do you feel? How does God feel about
you? Let God respond to your still very young freedom as God chooses. Then you might ponder God's
word to you as spoken through Isaiah:

*You are precious in my eyes. . . . I give whole worlds for
you.* —Isaiah 43:4

This prayer exercise of looking at God looking at us steadily and tenderly is one which we can return to over and over
again with the confidence that God loves us just the way we are.
God remembers that we are dust, and, like the good-enough parent, celebrates our ordinary efforts to be our true self, the good
and bad, the weak and the strong, our missing the mark as well
as making it.

God understands and appreciates our anger. For an adult
who grew up in a dysfunctional family the expression of anger
may feel very risky. If expressions of anger were out of control,
wild, violent, or personally abusive, our fear of anger may be
especially vivid. Expressions of anger which ridiculed, silenced,
and iced all conversation could be equally frightening. Our angry
feelings, however, are meant not to destroy nor even to hurt, but
to serve as useful messages to ourselves about our needs and the
violations of our boundaries.

Our anger may *feel* like the hurricane force of a three-year-old's all-out tantrum. The *expression* of our anger, however, need not be abusive, punitive, destructive if we can talk the anger through with a safe person; as we calm we may role-play with that safe person, practicing how to communicate it to the offender, if indeed it is safe to do so. If it doesn't even feel safe to talk it through with a human person, we might ask God to listen to our rage. God can listen to it and to us, even in our wild fury, our violent desires. God has a long history with psalmists who cursed—frequently.

Many childhood events may have left us filled with anger. Perhaps family circumstances prevented our receiving some of the ordinary emotional supplies and modeling to grow securely into adulthood. Perhaps our anger is more muted, a growing discontent, an annoying vulnerability to being easily irritated or disappointed.

> Whatever the shape and depth of your anger, try to externalize it. Try to name it, paint it, or shape it with clay. Try a dance of anger. Then hold this treasure before God who is happy to receive it—and you. Yes, you, even angry.

Another way in which God can reparent the frantic heart is to "set the strong and healthy out to play" (Ezekiel 34:16). In some translations, although the Hebrew word is missing from the original text, we read that the strong and the healthy God will destroy. Which is the more truthful image of God's action as we grow stronger and more healthy? There is one sure way to know, even though there is no verb in the original manuscript. We look to Jesus. Would Jesus destroy the healthy or set them out to play? Jesus comes that we might have life—not life eked out or measured out gram by gram, but life in abundance (John 10:10). Jesus enjoys setting us out to play.

The frantic heart has almost as much difficulty with play as with anger. Stifled perhaps in the important child-work of play, required to color inside the lines or squelched in our normal creativity and exploration, we may never have learned to play with spontaneity. Perhaps we learned too early that working or taking care of parental needs won more approval than our playing.

> The Spirit prays within us (Romans 8:15, 26) and plays within us. Let bubble up images, memories, and feelings which are playful—and simple.

> Make a list of ten or fifteen things you like to do.

> Is money necessary for these enjoyable activities of yours to become real? Must you have other people involved or is this play possible even alone? What are you waiting for . . . ? "I will play before the Lord" (Psalm 100).

To pray is to play. Play the psalms, make music to our God! Playfulness is a sign of a healing heart. To play is to have flexibility and freedom. We forget everything but the moment when we are caught by play. We have a shift of perspective. Israel played before the Lord. Jesus played, and not just as a child. Notice how he moves from the landlocked hills of Nazareth to the seashore town of Capernaum. Was it swimming he loved? Boating? He wandered among the lilies of the field and played with children. If God could sing and dance for joy over God's people (Zephaniah 3:16–20), picture the image of God in the flesh tucking up his robe and throwing back his head. His sandals slap the earth! Jesus prays.

Now, having fixed your eyes on Jesus, playing as an adult, enjoying his simple self and the simple gifts of life, return to the last exercise and again let the Spirit play in your heart.

Jesus and the Frantic Heart

Jesus is attracted to the busy.

She gathered up the burial cloths and was about to grab the bucket to go for well water. Jesus touched her arm. "Let that go," he suggested. "I need to take a walk. Come with me, Martha, please." They left the group gathered in awe around Lazarus, whom Jesus had just called out of the tomb—alive again.

She smiled. She loved being singled out. Her parents so many years ago had told her she was the smartest of their three, so responsible, serious, practical. "Too bad you were not a boy," her father had lamented. Her mother had died when she was just five, and her father came to rely heavily on her. She supervised the two little ones, made the meals, did the marketing, and fetched the water supply until Mary was big enough to manage the bucket. The market and meals she never turned over. Martha was in charge.

Aunt Ruth had taught her to weave when she was just six. Now she was noted even in Jerusalem for her skills as a weaver. A bitter memory tinged her recollection. Skill had not been enough for Jacob. He had been proud to marry her, to wear her like an ornament around town, to boast about her to his merchant mates in Jerusalem. That had been before the death of their infant son. Martha had been outraged. How could God do this to her? She was, although no woman need be, a strict observer of the law, a woman of prayer and duty. She deserved better from God, and told God so frequently, at the top of her lungs.

Jacob's resentment was quiet, smoldering, erupting now and then into bitterness with her. They tried to conceive, and sometimes she miscarried. Martha could imagine her fate. After ten years of marriage the law allowed Jacob to divorce her. He must have a son, and she had failed. She cooked so well, sewed so beautifully, showed such talent in their small garden. Why had God closed her womb? She had been so good, so faithful to the law, and now the law would strip her bare.

She was a realistic woman. Indeed, on their tenth wedding anniversary Jacob had the divorce papers drawn up, and then formally cast her out. Law, the damned law, said she must return to her father's house. But her precious father, who had admired her so, also could see where Jacob and Martha's marriage was headed by its ninth year and had died then, grieving for his favorite child, his helpmate.

She had turned to Lazarus, her baby brother, a strapping lively man of twenty. No matter that his own young wife had died two years ago in childbirth. Once the young man had settled his two older sisters, for Mary had been divorced the same year for making a continual mess of her husband's meals, Lazarus could always search for a new wife.

In fact, it was while he had been on that search that he had met Jesus and had invited him home for dinner. What a night that had been! Martha had organized almost a banquet for the charming teacher from Galilee. She would shine again. Her meal, her mastery, would be the centerpiece.

Not that Mary could cook. It just made Martha seethe to see Mary the center of the teacher's attention. Well, she could always control Mary with a raised eyebrow. "Mary!" Her call carried a demand. Mary never noticed the arched eyebrow. "Master," Martha cried, appealing to the social customs, "do you not care that Mary has left all the work to me?" He smiled. "Martha, Martha, you are so busy. Just make one dish, a simple supper. Mary is eager to learn from me, and I want you here with me, too."

She had been flustered. No man had every wanted her to listen and learn. That was only for male Jews. She could not impress him with her scurrying to lay a fine table. How would she then be special to him?

Over the months she came to trust that she and her family were special to Jesus. She asked him to come when Lazarus fell deathly ill, and when He did not arrive, her world, her security collapsed. Jesus did not care. Lazarus was dead. Mary was exhausted with grief, but Martha concealed her fear with rage.

"Where were you?" she screamed at Jesus. Jesus stood on the road where she had raced to meet him. She hurtled herself at him in fury. Only social custom kept her from moving too close and beating on his chest. Her fists and her heart clenched. They were friends. She was entitled to his help. Her words—bitter, sarcastic, raging, terror-stricken torrents—made him wince. Her pain etched his face.

"Martha, my dearest Martha." She could not hear him, but he could wait. When her shoulders finally slumped and the tears began, he moved to hold her. "No!" she cried, and stiffened. She stood alone then, sobbing and shaking. So very alone.

Finally she took a small step toward him. He gathered her in his arms, and after a long silence he reassured her. "Nothing is lost. There is hope." She was collapsing more and more into him, slowly relaxing, hoping again.

She shook herself free. She had responsibilities. Mary. The mourners from Jerusalem. "Come along, Jesus." She raced ahead. "Mary," she called, "the Master is asking for you." He had not, but she knew he would have if she had not created such a scene. She was definitely in charge.

In charge of Lazarus, too. "Get washed," she ordered her newly raised brother, once the burial cloths had been unwrapped. She was just going for more water when Jesus wanted to go for a walk. What a strange man, she mused. He should be glorying in this great deed and he wants to go off—and with me.

They moved away from the house together. "I never said thank you. I'm so very grateful, Jesus." He smiled, "Thank God, Martha. God loves you so dearly because you are so needy." She flinched. "Hardly," she retorted, her lips pursed in disdain.

"Very needy, very small, very lonely, working so hard to help, to be noticed, to be cared for in a tit-for-tat way. God doesn't do tit-for-tat, Martha. The righteous have it all totaled up and seem to have no need for God. What happened on the road today was a revelation that you are not entitled, you do not deserve, you cannot claim. God is free, Martha.

"You tried to possess me today, too, Martha, to make me pay you back for all your fine meals." His eyes twinkled. "You do try to control others just as rigidly as you try to control yourself. Today your control failed you. You were so very real. Oh, how I do love you, Martha!"

"You love me when I was hating you, wanting to do violence to you, more angry than I have ever been?"

"I love you, Martha, not a wooden woman so afraid of her spontaneity and emotions and needs. Your passion is beautiful. Please, please, let yourself flow, Martha. Trust God to take charge. Just laugh and love and leave Lazarus and Mary just as free to be as you are going to let me be. You are going to let me be free, Martha?"

She flung her head back and laughed; then, social custom to the winds, she hugged him to her heart.

Martha is you . . .
Jesus responds to your hug by . . .

Part 3

The Holy Heart

The place on which you stand is holy ground.
—Exodus 3:5

In this last chapter, we will look briefly at some of the graces we pray for in the wholing of the heart, very ordinary gifts which are given, neither grasped at nor "worked at" as "shoulds." Frequently we have remembered that healing is a process, ordinarily not an event. Healing and wholing of our hearts seems to happen one day at a time, just as the twelve-step programs so wisely remind us.

The Grace of the Ordinary

So it is with the graces for which we pray, these simple gifts, the grace of the ordinary. They are given one day at a time and, like all ordinary human development, in a spiraling rather than linear fashion. The more ordinary we become, it seems, the holier we are made, shaped by grace. Grace is the expression of God's freedom, God's own life—nothing we can earn or deserve.

In the earlier chapters we have invited God to touch painful—frozen, hungry, frantic—places, the holes in our hearts. Whatever your life experience is, or has been, God "has been carrying you as a man carries his child all along your journey until you arrived at this place" (Deuteronomy 1:31).

The *shalom,* the wholeness for which we pray, is threefold: the ordinary graces of acceptance, compassion, and gratitude. We ask to accept our true self; then acceptance of others just as they are, in their truth, will flow. We ask to offer compassion, first to ourselves as flawed and frail, so that compassion for others with their limits and liabilities will grow. We ask for gratitude, for who we were, are, and are becoming, so that someday we may be grateful for all and everyone, trusting that "all will be well, all manner of thing will be well" (Julian of Norwich).

Acceptance

God, grant me the serenity to accept the things I cannot change, the courage to change the things I can, and the wisdom to know the difference.

This foundational prayer of the twelve-step programs holds part of what we ask for.

In the movement from the frozen heart to the feeling heart, we gradually allow awareness to tell us about reality. As we become more able to recognize and take in the juice and ordinary joys of human living we are able to become more courageous in making the changes we need to make. These changes may be simply a deepened awareness of nature, of relationship, and of balanced work—a greater sense of feeling grounded as a "child of the universe." Or it may mean the courageous move away from an abusive situation, of taking one step at a time to change a situation. In a dysfunctional family, the grace of acceptance invites us to let go of denial and try to name the truth of our situation however painful that might be. Having named the truth, at least some of its bits and pieces, the grace who is Spirit nudges us to take the tiny steps toward shaping our reality in a more human way. "My heart is ready, O God, my heart is ready" (Psalm 57:8).

Compassion

In the movement from the hungry heart to the receiving heart there is a deepening of a genuine compassion. One of the ways we might sum up Jesus' way of being in the world is compassionate action. The gospel stories give us fleshed out pictures of this compassionate presence and action over and over again.

Our hungry hearts sometimes get confused about compassion. The "wisdom to know the difference," for the person whose heart-boundaries are not clear helps to determine the difference between genuine compassion for self and others and co-dependent caretaking, even enabling others to continue their self-destructive behaviors. If indiscriminate caretaking to the point of exhaustion or feeling victimized (and then self-righteous) has been our way of being and doing, we need to be converted from this goodness which can leave our hearts not only weary but secretly judgmental and bitter.

By compassionating our own human limits and being respectful of our own legitimate needs, our hearts become more capable of genuine compassionate action for others. In the process of receiving and becoming our true self we grow in our ability to be with others and for others, in our family, our community, and the global community of the world. We do not become a self for the sake of narcissistic isolation and gratification. We become more and more *response-able* to the needs of our various "families" instead of assuming unrealistic responsibility for others' feelings and problems.

Gratitude

As we slow down and move from frantic maneuvers for approval to the simple truth of who we and others are, our capacity for gratitude deepens and widens. Instead of requiring others to replenish our meager store of self-esteem by their affirmation, approval, and appreciation, we grow grateful for others, for who they are, neither larger-than-life nor beneath us, but ordinary persons like ourselves. As we learn to feel less entitled we are surprised over and over again by the ordinary joys and gifts of every day—a beautiful sunset, a smile, a baked potato drenched in sour cream. Our new tolerance of ourselves as ordinary people spills over into a new appreciation for others. We stop being like Lucy in the cartoon strip "Peanuts" who shrieks: "I don't want life to have up's and down's. I just want *up's* and *upper-up's* and *upper-upper-up's!*" We become more comfortable with the ebb and flow of life.

Everything Is Grace

As we grow more accepting, compassionate, and grateful, we are on the journey of coming home to ourselves. This process of homecoming provides glimmers of an amazing reality: everything is grace. It was a simple man, the hero in Georges Bernanos' novel *Diary of a Country Priest*, who saw this truth. He who was hardly pollyanna but *"un homme mangé,"* a man eaten, voices how we can know moments, at the core of ourselves, that, in surviving, even our pain has taught us. We come to know and to accept that our one and only life is good, that in everything we can praise and thank God.

Many persons whose childhood has left them with holes in their heart, however, grow up with depression as a too familiar companion. Functioning more or less efficiently, they know too well the foggy, smothering miasma of depressed feelings which rob them of joy and delight in the ordinary pleasures of life. They get along; sometimes even those closest do not know the inner grayness, the leaden feeling of running a race in two-ton sneakers. The self-doubts and guilts of depression, unknown or unreal to the eye of the outside beholder, inflict enormous pain.

The psalmist was no stranger to these feelings.

> *For my days are vanishing like smoke, my bones, smoldering like logs, my heart shriveling like scorched grass and my appetite has gone.* —Psalm 102:3–4

> *Save me, God! The water is already up to my neck! I am sinking in the deepest swamp, there is no foothold; I have stepped into deep water and the waves are washing over me.* —Psalm 69:1–2

What poignant metaphors for the anguish of depression.

And where is God in all of this? We finally discover and celebrate that God is in our tears, our heartache. In some mysterious way, as our own suffering makes us become more understanding and caring, we can enter into the pain of another with gentleness and attentiveness and genuine feeling-with. In some mysterious yet achingly familiar and down-to-earth way we become the heartache of God. Although we can barely understand and hardly dare to trust, our own experience opens us to the pain of others in ways which can be healing and wholing for them.

A very effective therapist, whose capacity for dealing with severely damaged persons is outstanding, can draw on her own struggle to be with others with a constancy reflecting the *'emet* of God. An accomplished educator, working through some of the pain of her own abused and lost childhood, is especially sensitive to some of the signals of distress in children, which no one was able to pick up from her so many years ago. Few of those with whom these two women work would guess the severe internal distress, anxiety, and depression which each has battled with over the years. The Word has been made flesh and dwells among us.

All of these graces—acceptance, compassion, and gratitude—can be gathered and named as the grace of homecoming. The quiet, familiar sense of being at home in our deepest self where God has always dwelt means being at home too with God. In this knowing we are home, we become more comfortable with the "rooms" of our house. We know the spaces which are light and airy, and the fabrics which are worn and tattered and need repair. We know that the attic and basement still contain unopened boxes and baggage from the past. Homecoming helps us to know that all is grace.

To come home to ourselves does not mean that we become strangers to the anxieties and depressions of our past. But their terror and control grows less and less as we become more at home in ourselves. It is a paradox that the most effective way to deal with that terrifying form of anxiety, the panic attack, is to let ourselves go into it, to be "at home" with those feelings which made Jesus himself sweat blood in the garden, knowing that we will emerge at the other end. The dizzying, throat-constricting, heart-hammering engulfment by anxiety, sometimes provoked by a specific situation or place, and sometimes unannounced, is an awesome but survivable storm. Its pounding, crashing surf is best ridden to shore than resisted and fought.

After exile, after anxiety that sometimes escalated into panic, and after depression that usually erupted into grief, Israel was carried home by God. Isaiah describes this great homecoming of God's people. We too are promised: "You shall be radiant . . . your heart shall throb and overflow" (Isaiah 60:4–5). As we grow more at home with our true selves and experience the heart-throbbings of being alive as good and holy, we discover that indeed our hearts do overflow. "My heart overflows with a lovely theme as I sing my song" to God (Psalm 45).

Empowering the Heart

To claim our own wholeness is to allow God to be more whole and holy in our lives. To be able to dialogue with God, wrestle with God, shake fists at God, scream at God, be tender with God, rejoice with God—to be all that it means to be human in range and in depth—makes us more real with God who is, yet who wants to be acknowledged as, the deepest reality at the heart of our self. To claim our own wholeness is to invite God to be all that God can be. God is holy. God wants us to be holy.

The word *holy* in Hebrew and Greek is a synonym for just. God's justice may have been taught in such a way as to terrorize us, especially if we were already feeling we had no right to exist. If such a vulnerable creature made even one false move—annihilation! God's just anger may have been used by family, teachers, and clergy to control not only our behavior but our thinking, wanting, and feeling.

Yet biblical justice is the foundation for love. We cannot love others as we love ourselves until we are as just toward others as we are to ourselves. As we grow in capacity to love ourselves, our capacity for justice also enlarges. Justice is so very basic. It is, in scripture, often linked with truth: "Justice and peace shall kiss and truth will spring up from the earth" (Psalm 85:11–12). In the first two sections of this book truth has been springing up from the earth, from the *humus*, the Latin word for soil, earth, ground, or dirt. This is our *human* condition, the truth about ourselves. As justice, truth and *shalom* embrace our lives, the Spirit is fostering us as human, re-creating us as whole, and empowering us as holy.

To be holy means to be just. Accepting our one and only life, grieving our lost childhood and the stifling of our true and human self, and understanding our own hearts and their holes with compassion are all ways to "let justice roll like a river" (Am 5:24). Hopefully we can begin to see our parents and families as human, not gods who disappoint nor demons who destroy. When we see how much we share in common with them, we can accept, be compassionate, and perhaps, eventually—but truthfully—be grateful for their offering us the best they could. We need power and energy for that kind of justice and holiness.

"Oh you slow of heart!" Jesus rebukes his friends on the way to Emmaus (Luke 24:25), then sets their hearts burning within them. We are indeed slow of heart, broken-hearted, half-hearted. Our hearts are empty, rejected, and isolated. They are hungry, craving, and addicted. They are frantic, whipped, and imprisoned. As Jesus opens our heart to the word—and the Word-made-flesh in the messy reality we call human living and loving—healing happens. As Jesus explains the scriptures of our own lives to us as we journey along together, healing happens. As we learn to accept the ambiguities of reality and the ambivalences of our lives and our loves, healing happens.

As healing happens, we become quick of heart. When we become quick of heart, we are alert, quick to pay attention to the holes in the lives of others beyond our parents and families. Justice impels us to be quick to notice the holes in the fabric of society. "Your own wound shall quickly be healed," God promises us even as we pass on, one day at a time, the freedom, the food, and the home which we have received. "Ancient ruins will be rebuilt" in our relationships (Isaiah 58:7–14), both personal and global. We need power and energy for that kind of justice and holiness. The power and energy of God's own Spirit quickens our hearts.

Power in Greek is *dynamis,* the energy of life. God's own energy is another name for Spirit in the New Testament. As we grow more and more able to turn our lives—past, present, and future—over to a "higher power," the "deeper energy" of God who is the Spirit empowers us to accept ourselves, our reality, and our relationships as they are. We are empowered to forgive ourselves and even to forgive God for the flaws and frailties of that reality; to compassionate ourselves, our families, and our communities for being human; to integrate the split-off parts of ourselves; to reconcile what is at war in our relationships; and to trust that God passionately desires and works for our integrity, our *shalom,* the wholing of our heart.

> *Glory be to God whose power at work in us can do infinitely more than we can ask or even imagine!*
> —Ephesians 4:20

Bibliography

Beattie, Melody, *Co-Dependent No More*. New York: Harper & Row, 1987.

Bernanos, Georges. *Diary of a Country Priest*. New York: Macmillan Company, 1937.

Bowlby, John. *Attachment and Loss*. 2 vols. (Vol. I: *Attachment*. Vol. II: (*Separation: Anxiety and Anger*.) New York: Basic Books, 1969, 1973.

Bradshaw, John. *On the Family*. Deerfield Beach: Health Communications, Inc., 1988.

———. *Healing the Shame That Binds*. Deerfield Beach: Health Communications, 1989.

Callahan, Rachel and Rea McDonnell. *God Is Close to the Brokenhearted: Good News for Those Who Are Depressed*. Cincinnati: St. Anthony Messenger Press, 1996.

———. *Hope for Healing: Good News for Adult Children of Alcoholics*. Dubuque: Islewest Publishers, 1998.

———. *Welcome Home: Healing Your Broken Heart*. (Audio tape) Cincinnati: St. Anthony Messenger Press, 1995.

Gill, Jean. *Unless You Become Like a Little Child*. Mahwah: Paulist, 1985.

Grassi, Joseph. *Healing the Heart*. Mahwah: Paulist, 1987.

Halpern, Howard. *How to Break Your Addiction to a Person*. New York: Bantam, 1982.

Johnson, Stephen. *Characterological Transformation*. New York: W. W. Norton & Company, 1985.

———. *Humanizing the Narcissistic Style*. New York: W. W. Norton & Company, 1987.

Jordan, Merle. *Taking on the Gods: The Task of the Pastoral Counselor*. Nashville: Abingdon Press, 1986.

Julian of Norwich. *Meditations*. Ed. Brendan Doyle. Santa Fe: Bear and Company, 1987.

Kaplan, Louise. *Oneness and Separateness: From Infant to Individual*. New York: Simon and Schuster, 1978.

Lerner, Harriet Goldhor. *The Dance of Anger.* New York: Harper & Row, 1985.

McDonnell, Rea. *When God Comes Close.* Boston: Daughters of St. Paul, 1994.

Miller, Alice. *The Drama of the Gifted Child.* New York: Basic Books, 1981.

Patton, John. *Is Human Forgiveness Possible?* Nashville: Abingdon Press, 1985.

Winnicott, D. W. "Ego Distortion in Terms of True and False Self." In *The Maturational Process and the Facilitating Environment.* Connecticut: International Universities Press, 1965.

Other Books By Islewest

OUR CHILDREN ARE ALCOHOLICS: Coping with Children Who Have Addictions
Sally and David B. $13.95
Our Children Are Alcoholics will provide relief and reassurance for troubled parents. The authors and other parents tell their own stories of how they found health and serenity in the midst of the chaos caused by the addictions of their children. They give hope to other parents along with their suggestions on how to deal with addicted children of any age. Includes an informative section on the nature of the disease and an extensive bibliography.

THERE'S MORE TO QUITTING DRINKING THAN QUITTING DRINKING
Dr. Paul O. $14.95
This book is for the recovering person who wants more than physical sobriety—who wants mental, emotional, interpersonal, and spiritual sobriety. Written in a bright, witty style, Dr. Paul presents a practical guide to enrich your journey through the "Land of Beginning Again."

THE TOAD WITHIN: How to Control Eating Choices
Dr. James Weldon Worth $12.95
Dr. Worth's mythical creation, the Toad, is a metaphor for our appetite when it becomes difficult to control. By envisioning our runaway appetite as a mischievous and persistent Toad, who bullies us with food temptations, we have an adversary that can be visualized, confronted, and captured. Dr. Worth shows us how to engage in imaginary struggles with our load and defeat him or her by choosing wisely and courageously. Humorous and Insightful!!!

WALKING ON EGGSHELLS: When Someone You Care About Has Borderline Personality Disorder
Paul Mason, MS, and Randi Kreger $11.95
Coping with the behaviors of Borderline Personality Disorder—rage, extreme inconsistency, verbal abuse, impulsiveness, self-mutilation, and black-and-white thinking—can be devastating. Those who must deal with a BP—parents, spouses, lovers, friends, teachers—need answers NOW. *Walking on Eggshells* was written to provide those

answers quickly and clearly. It is a book of survival and empowerment for people who care about someone with BPD.

THROUGH THE INNER EYE: Awakening to the Creative Spirit
Jan Groenemann $19.95
The inner self is the key to wholeness. Explore the expression of self as you are guided beyond self-imposed boundaries and reach within to your true self. Extraordinary examples of full-color art and poetry illustrate the process used to help individuals get in touch with their inner lives. Abundant activities and exercises lead individuals to find more passion, purpose, and productivity in their lives as they become free, creative, and whole.

RIGHT SIDE UP! Reflections for Those Living with Serious Illness
Marlene Halpin $10.95
One reflection per page makes this book manageable for those who are unable to focus for prolonged periods. The clarity and warmth of Ms. Halpin's poems and photos portray a sense of peace and well-being. **A Perfect Gift!**

SWALLOWED BY A SNAKE: The Gift of the Masculine Side of Healing
Thomas R. Golden, LCSW $13.95
Golden explains why most current grief therapy suits women better than men and how the genders differ in their approach to healing. The accepted mode of healing relies primarily on verbal and emotional expressions—comfortable for many women and alien to many men. He illustrates the role grief plays across time and cultures, and provides many examples of healing strategies.

HUNGER OF THE HEART: Communion at the Wall
Larry Powell $19.95
A powerful photo documentation of the **healing impact** that the Vietnam Veterans Memorial has on those who journey there. Powell offers a unique historical record of life at the Wall. His poignant photographs remind us that for thousands of suffering souls, their war is not over.

SEE WHAT I'M SAYING: What Children Tell Us Through Their Art
Dr. Myra Levick, Ph.D $15.95
Is your child in good emotional health? Struggling with a problem? Typical for his or her age? Dr. Levik says that the answers to all these

questions can be seen in how and what your child draws. A leader in the field of Art Therapy, Levik gives expert help in understanding what children communicate through their drawings, and offers practical tools for assessing a child's intellectual and emotional development.

THEY DO REMEMBER: A Story of Soul Survival
Sandy Robins $13.95
A story of survival, recovery, and hope for victims of abuse. This poignant autobiography will help abuse victims and survivors realize they do have a choice; they can move from trauma to understanding and healing.

DOUBLE JEOPARDY: Treating Juvenile Victims and Perpetrators for the Dual Disorder of Sexual Abuse and Substance Abuse
Chris Frey, MSW, LCSW $36.95
It has become common for clients in treatment to present both childhood sexual abuse and substance abuse experiences. *Double Jeopardy* is a highly successful dual disorder treatment program, originally developed for Boys Town of Missouri, that leads to a reduction in the rate of relapse.

THERE'S A SPOUSE IN THE HOUSE: Get 'Em Out
Patricia Schnepf $5.95
Do you have a spouse in the house going through the throes of retirement? Let *There's a Spouse in the House* help you and your spouse make the transition to retirement a creative and adventurous time in your life. This resource will help you make the rest of your life the BEST of your life as you discover a variety of ways to redirect your time, talent, and resources.

MEN AT WORK: An Action Guide to Masculine Healing
Chris Frey, MSW, LCSW $14.95
This book helps readers free themselves from worn-out notions of what it means to be a man. It provides an action-oriented approach to healing work, within the combined context of mind, body, and spirit. Practical, down-to-earth, and broadly based. It is written for men who want to heal their lives, men and women who want to better understand a loved one, and for therapists who are working with men. May be utilized by the reader on his or her own, in therapy groups, and in self-help support groups.

BEYOND THE BLAME GAME: Creating Compassion and Ending the Sex War in Your Life
Dmitri Bilgere $10.95
Become a savvy CO (conscientious objector) in the war between the sexes. Dmitri Bilgere shows you how to stop unconsciously stimulating the behaviors you hate most in the opposite sex and how to encourage behaviors you value. Learn how to untangle yourself from the blame game and see your relationships improve instantly and permanently.

THE PEACEFUL SOUL WITHIN: Reflective Steps Toward Awareness
Margot Robinson $14.95
The pain you suffer can make you a victim or a winner. Margot Robinson teaches you to use the pain in your life as a means of transforming loss, failure, and even despair into joyful self-acceptance and inner peace. Her down-to-earth reflections and practical exercises demonstrate how to take control and responsibility for your own happiness.

FROM THE HEARTS OF MEN
Yevrah Ornstein $16.95
Within the hearts of men lie secret yearnings, needs, and fears that have long been held captive by the taboos of society. The authentic voices in this book, and the magnificent spirit that ennobles them cry out to be heard. Read them and your view of men will never be the same.

FORGING NEW FATHERS: Why Contemporary Fatherhood Must Change
Yevrah Ornstein $12.95
Unnoticed, unheard, unsung—fathers are changing. Ornstein explores the changes taking place as men push aside the gates of isolation and dispassion and enter into heartfelt involvement in family life. Drawing upon the voices of a variety of men, he gives fathers an opportunity to tell their stories. They tackle hard questions, including what its like to be a single, surrogate, custodial or non-custodial parent? *Forging New Fathers* gives voice to a perspective long ignored—that of fathers themselves—and it does so in honest, intimate terms, which may radically change the reader's view of dads.

TALKING WITH OUR BROTHERS: Creating and Sustaining a Dynamic Men's Group
George M. Taylor $9.50
Taylor explains why men need groups, how men's groups work, why some men's groups fail, and how to start a group. The heart of the book is devoted to dozens of detailed exercises, for use in group settings. Topics include exploration of gender roles, shame, touching, grief, racism, work, body image, forgiveness, and intimacy. Each exercise is laid out in step-by-step format, with helpful comments and advice. Anyone planning to start, lead, or participate in a men's group would profit from this sound, practical advice.

RESTORING AMERICA'S FUTURE
Gene Gordon $9.95
Gordon, a highly successful architect, engineer, and businessman, offers concrete, fundamental solutions—that have been used successfully by independent businesses—to help our country become once again a financially secure world leader.

**To Place a Credit Card Order Call
1-800-557-9867
Mention this ad for free shipping.**